THE SALES WAR

HOW TO DOMINATE YOUR
MARKETPLACE WITHOUT SACRIFICING
YOUR BODY, YOUR MARRIAGE,
YOUR CHILDREN, OR YOUR SOUL

BRIAN Q. DAVIS

Written in Laguna Beach, CA, Dallas, TX and Goldeneye, Ocho Rios, Jamaica.

'I rewrote nothing and made no corrections until my book was finished,' he said. 'If I had looked back at what I had written the day before I might have despaired at the mistakes in grammar and style, the repetitions and the crudities. And I obstinately closed my mind to self-mockery and "what will my friends say?" I savagely hammered on until the proud day when the last page was done."

- Ian Fleming, on writing Casino Royale

www.thesaleswar.com

SYNDICATE EDITION V2

Printed in USA

Print ISBN: 979-8-98619-3-502
eBook ISBN: 979-8-98619-3-519

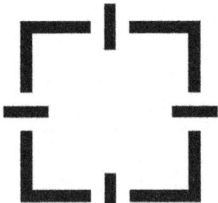

WARNING

This book is not for everyone.

This book is for high performers, sales producers, creators, and rainmakers.

It's for the man who smashes sales targets in the marketplace. He is admired by his peers and brings home big commissions and bonuses. He's been selling for years and knows the game. He often feels like he is carrying the company on his back. He is singularly focused on one thing: hunting down the number.

But, he also carries a background sense that *he* is the one being hunted. He pushes people away and buries himself with the work. Even when he's surrounded by colleagues, prospects, clients, and his family, he feels alone.

Is this you? If so, I know exactly how you feel.

It never mattered what industry I was in; I could sell. I spent the last twenty years in business-to-business sales and customer development. I changed the trajectories of my clients and employers. I sold across diverse industries, including aerospace, enterprise software, digital marketing, and healthcare. I generated the big numbers, the big clients, and the big moves that created value in the marketplace and millions of dollars in revenue. But, there was a feeling that was deep and suppressed. I knew there was something wrong with my world.

After years of grinding and selling, I realized it was *never going to be enough*.

The cycle of "never enough" was slowly killing me. My identity and significance as a salesperson were wrapped up in a lie so deep that I was blind to the pain and guilt that I was carrying.

Then, I woke up to the secret war that I was fighting. This hidden conflict exists across the sales profession and among entrepreneurs. There is a war with a false idol that destroys everything for the men who worship at its feet.

This book is a map to help you identify and destroy the idol that has you silently in its grip. In the chapters that follow, you will learn how to dominate your marketplace, *without* sacrificing your body, your marriage, your children, or your soul.

Keep reading, and we'll dominate the marketplace together.

You are no longer alone.

Wake up.

CONTENTS

Chapter 1: THE LIE 1

Chapter 2: THE TRUTH 11

WELCOME TO WEAPONS TRAINING 19

Chapter 3: THE WEAPON OF THE SPIRIT 21

Chapter 4: THE WEAPON OF THE HEART 39

Chapter 5: THE WEAPON OF THE BODY 67

Chapter 6: THE WEAPON OF PRESENCE 89

Chapter 7: WIELDING THE WEAPON OF PRESENCE...... 105

Chapter 8: WINNING THE SALES WAR 141

Bonus: THE FORMULA FOR GUARANTEED RESULTS.... 151

Bonus: LEAD WHAT YOU LIVE 155

WEAPONS AND RESOURCES 159

GRATITUDE AND ACKNOWLEDGEMENTS 164

DEDICATION 167

SPECIAL THANKS 169

CHAPTER 1

THE LIE

THE LIE

I only wanted one thing: to win The Salesman of The Year Award. This coveted title was given to the top salesperson at an extravagant ceremony at the end of the year. You probably have a similar award at your company.

I was approaching the end of my second year at the company, but I still felt like a new guy who had something to prove. The executive team had brought me and a few others in to "shake up the O.G. sales team" because revenue growth for the company had plateaued. I was tasked with selling digital marketing services and technology to the bureaucratic beast also known as the American healthcare industry. It was a new marketplace for me, and I didn't have any foundational relationships or even any industry knowledge to build from. Still, I was committed to doing *whatever it would take* to bring home the award. In my heart, that award would be the thing that would confirm that I had been a good choice for the mission.

So I played the game as an underdog with a huge chip on my shoulder. I defaulted back to the tactic that had always produced results during my rugby career: *just outwork everyone*. So I spent seventy days on the road away from my pregnant wife and one-year-old daughter selling to hospital systems all over the country. There was no meeting I would not take and no end to the effort I would commit. Of course, my strategy produced results. I finished the fourth quarter as the top sales producer in the company and closed the biggest single deal in company history.

But, for the first time in the company's history, there was no awards ceremony. The company had grown and the event was judged to be too expensive. There would be no naming of the Salesman of the Year on the big stage with all the company fanfare. The one target I had focused on all year was not only canceled, but it no longer existed. In fact, at the last minute, on the last sales day of the year, I got an email saying that the contest that I had dedicated everything to winning would serve everyone better if it was declared a tie with a salesman from a different division.

"A tie?" I thought. What was this?

I rubbed my eyes, looked up at the sky, and asked, "What the hell?" Didn't they know how much I had sacrificed?

I sat there alone on my front steps in Dallas, TX, on January 1, 2017, with nothing to show for all of the sacrifices I had made. There was no significance. There was no recognition. There were no awards. Nothing.

I was forty pounds overweight. I had sacrificed three and a half months away from home during my daughter's second year of life. I was filled with rage and contempt. There I sat. Empty. I felt worthless without the recognition of that award. And, in the midst of my depression and anger, I was completely oblivious to the fact I had a second daughter arriving in just six weeks.

Deep in my mind, an unspoken question emerged: "If I didn't have the sales awards to show, what was my worth?"

The chip on my shoulder got bigger. In identity crisis mode, I called my sales mentor and asked him what I should do. He told me that my theme for 2017 should be "to leave no doubt."

He saw an opportunity to poke my ego, and he did. Hard. His words helped immediately reignite all of the determination to win and prove myself. The only thing more impressive than setting an all-time sales record was to do *it twice in a row.*

I started planning how I was going to beat the record again.

I spent a furious month of January booking on-site client meetings for the first quarter of the year. When I got to an in-person meeting, I had an 80-90% win rate, so getting on the road was my plan. Just get me in front of the customer.

By the time the third week of February rolled around, I had booked eight out of the next ten weeks with travel to see prospects and clients. It was all lining up! I was going to smash last year's numbers. To hell with the bullshit awards. To hell with our competitors. I was going to take their clients away and put them out of business. I was going to crush anything that was in my way of the target.

I would "leave no doubt" about who was the greatest salesman at the company.

What I failed to realize was that the rage and contempt I felt at the company was really anger at myself. I would soon wake up to this reality amid the cries of a baby who had a birth defect that was soon to be discovered.

Feb 19, 2017, Methodist Dallas Medical Center, Dallas, TX 10:42 PM

I had only caught a quick glimpse of Perry when she arrived. She had a head full of dark hair. She was beautiful.

But then, as they were wrapping her up in a pink blanket, I noticed something was strange with her feet.

Her feet were bent at odd angles. I rubbed my eyes, questioning if what I was seeing was real. Her ankles had a purple hue to them and looked...broken. Was I the only one who noticed?

My heart rose in my chest in a wave of initial panic. What was wrong with her feet?

As they placed Perry on Susanna's chest, the doctor passed by, and I asked if she noticed the baby's feet.

"Oh. That's just bilateral clubfeet. Don't worry about it. They'll fix it," she said quietly, and then she resumed her duties in the chaos of the post-birth operations.

"What the hell are bilateral clubfeet?" I thought to myself. Fear flooded in. All I had were questions: Is she in pain? Can she walk? Will she be able to run? Will she need surgery? What is this going to mean for our family? How can I tell Susanna? Should I tell her now?

Perry was peaceful and happy despite her feet and ankles that looked like they were broken.

I had no idea of the Divine Message she was carrying for me.

---

9 Days Later: Feb 28, 2017, 12:35 AM

My eyes hurt, and I had that sick adrenaline feeling in my stomach. I sat at my home office desk that was wedged in our master bedroom and stared at the PowerPoint deck on my laptop screen. I was making final adjustments to the exhaustive presentation that I was going to use for the first of my big sales meetings that I had scheduled. Perry was in pain in the next room. Susanna was trying to get her to sleep, but she had been crying for 12 hours straight. Earlier that morning, the doctors had applied the first set of plaster casts to begin treatment of both of her clubfeet feet. They told us she had at least three years of casts and braces in her future. This evening was the first day of her treatment. She had been crying with such intensity that her tiny voice was becoming hoarse.

I started to panic that I wouldn't be prepared for the presentation the next afternoon. I was flying to Virginia from Texas in the morning to pitch to a large physician's group. Perry's crying was relentless. She was in so much pain, and we had no way of helping her.

Then I heard another sound.

Susanna started to cry as her endurance gave out.

"How the fuck and I am I going to get this sales deck done with all this noise?" I thought.

My exhaustion from lack of sleep, anxiety over the sales presentation, and the mental stress of hearing my family in pain broke me. Frustration. Anger. Rage. I slammed my laptop screen shut and exploded into the next room where Susanna was rocking Perry.

"CAN WE SHUT THE FUCK UP?! SHUT THE FUCK UP!" I screamed.

Susanna looked up at me, shocked, tears streaming down her face. Perry's cries intensified.

Time stopped.

Susanna's blue eyes were red with exhaustion and tears. She looked at me like she was looking at a violent intruder in her house. She slowly stood up from her chair, cradling Perry in her arms, and backed away into the adjacent room.

I walked to the dark bathroom, flipped on the light, and looked in the mirror.

I did not recognize the man looking back at me. He was a monster.

His face was swollen. There were dark circles under his eyes. The weight of shame and guilt and sedation hung on his body, and his gut pushed out the bottom of his shirt.

Then a question came into my mind.

"Who the fuck am I?"

The man in the mirror could not be present for a new mother and a baby in pain. He had just unleashed rage at his wife when she was at her most vulnerable. Instead of protecting, loving, and supporting them, he had betrayed their trust and brought venom out of his own anxiety. They needed bread and what they got was stone. He was not the righteous Christian man, the good husband, the great dad, the bad-ass salesman he pretended to be. He was a sedated man, a liar, and a fake.

My daughter didn't have her father's presence. My wife didn't have her husband's support. They cried alone. The emperor had no clothes, and he was full of shit. He also had a plane to catch in a few hours.

Somewhere in the darkness of the house, Perry's cries continued.

Over the next several weeks of business travel, my wife dealt with the reality of Perry getting new casts from her toes to her thighs each week. The doctors bent her feet and ankles a little bit more and set them in new casts at every visit. Each week was twenty-four hours of pain for Perry, and often, Susanna would have to deal with it alone. I missed many of the appointments because of all the sales presentations I'd booked. After all, I was doing all of this for them!

One of the trips took me to our headquarters in California and I found myself getting fitted for a new custom suit. It turned out that there was a bit of recognition from the company after all. It was a gift for a job well done the previous year. I had never had a custom suit before, and this tailor worked with many celebrities and professional athletes. I had played rugby for seventeen seasons after college, so I was used to getting the "athletic-fit" suits.

But the problem with suit fittings is that it requires two things: a lot of looking in the mirror and gathering facts.

"Your shoulders are slumped," said the tailor. "And you've got more of a "pear shape," so we'll adjust for that."

Gut punch.

"You'll look great in this pinstripe. It will be really thinning."

There was no escaping reality. My body had morphed from a once lean, fit, and strong rugby player into a swollen businessman with a dad-bod. My physical being was just a representation of my spiritual condition. I was slumped under the weight of the suppressed guilt and shame of the disconnection from my family.

I left the tailors with that sick adrenaline feeling in my stomach again.

I had another flight to catch.

CHAPTER 2

THE TRUTH

THE TRUTH

Waking up to the Truth hurts. Facing the Truth hurts even more.

Perry's cries had woken me up to my painful reality, but it took a hell-week-like training event called "Warrior Week" to force me to truly face the truth in my own life. It was a massive pattern interrupt in my life that forced me to stop hiding and lying. I'll share more on that painful experience in the following chapters, but it created the space necessary to see the truth about my life as a salesman:

I was an idol worshiper.

To worship an idol is to seek certainty, to find certainty in anything other than God. Scripture warns over and over against this. It's the first of the Ten Commandments! I was worshiping the idol of being "Salesman of the Year." I was worshiping the idol of being at the top of the sales board and praying for recognition. I was worshiping the commission checks and bonuses.

I was sacrificing my body, my marriage, my children, and my soul at the feet of the idol of the number.

Perhaps you are too?

I see you at the airports. You may be reading this book on a flight to your next meeting. Perhaps it's your fourth day in a row of travel and meetings and hotels. Perhaps it's the fourth day you haven't seen or meaningfully connected with your family. Perhaps it will be the fourth night in a row having drinks with the customer and "dialing it up."

How do you feel?

Who do you see when you really look in the mirror?

If you feel trapped in this war, you're not alone, but there is a way to win. I'm going to give you the new weapons that I found during my fight.

But before we can get to any weapons, we first have to address the lie that is at the heart of why we worship idols in the first place:

"I am not enough."

SETTING UP THE IDOL

"I want my salespeople to have lots of debt. I want them hungry."

I remember hearing those words from a hardened, old school, chain-smoking sales manager during my first year in sales. I was working at an engineering software and hardware reseller in Southern California. We sold into aerospace and automotive companies. It was a hard-charging, blue-collar sales environment. We had an intense competition with other resellers and other software companies on every deal.

The chain-smoking sales manager revealed everything about the nature of most sales organizations and the frame[1] that many companies are looking to put on their sales team.

The system is set up to keep you in a position of scarcity. Just like the chain-smoking sales manager, most companies operate from a place of fear and scarcity and a lack of trust in their sales forces at large. Companies know that the vast majority of people will drive themselves harder because of the fear of pain rather than the desire for

---

1. You will find the use of the word "frame" throughout this book. It's an important concept to be aware of if you are not. In our context, a "frame" is anything that causes a person or others to react to it. I.e., "The salesperson gave an amazing presentation and held everyone's attention. He really owned the *frame*".

pleasure. Thus the frame of the idol is set up. Impossible sales numbers are deployed. Quotas that are always just out of reach. Bonuses and targets that move. Activity monitoring and micromanagement. The idol's iron grip around your throat.

When a high producer steps into this framework, he finds it repulsive, and he hates the idea of being forced into a box that someone else controls. His ego counter-attacks:

"I'll crush these numbers."

"I'll do the biggest numbers anyone has ever done."

Driven by ego and scarcity, the game then becomes about taking down the numbers **at all costs**. The idol worship has begun, and casualties start mounting.

Time with family is negotiable. Connection to family and God disappears. His body degrades. Weight is gained. Addictions begin. Shame and guilt arrive along with results in the sales numbers. The success in business reinforces that this way of living works, and the man doubles down, buries the shame and guilt that accompanies disconnection and sedation, and the cycle repeats.

Q1. Q2. Q3. Q4. SALESMAN OF THE YEAR! TOP PRODUCER! Massive dose of perceived Significance. Power. Love. Connection.

The clock resets. The scoreboard goes to zero. It starts again.

The man finds himself in a loop where the ONLY place he can now find significance, power, love, and connection is in making more sales. His connection with himself is dead. His connection with his family withers. He can't hear God speaking to him anymore because of layers of shame and guilt of what he had to do to make the numbers.

Prospects and customers start to smell the stench of this virus of scarcity on him. This man eventually burns out, his performance falls apart, and the company replaces him.

His relentless effort to "be enough" and fill the growing spiritual emptiness inside himself fails.

Idols always betray the worshiper.

My chain-smoking sales manager would die of a heart attack a few years later.

THE TRUTH

The truth is that we cannot control much in business. We can only control our energy, action, and *what or who* we worship. *Sales, at its core, is an energetic game.* The salesman who brings the highest energetic resonance to the marketplace will always win.

He attracts business because he is a truth-teller. He hides nothing. He is connected to God. He is connected to his family. His body is a weapon. His energy allows him to hold space when others collapse. He connects where others cannot. He tells the truth when others lie.

His path to winning is through connection in his body, with his family, and with divine guidance. He is a man with nothing to hide.

He *owns the frame on himself.* His own targets are bigger than any quota anyone could assign him because they are heart-driven. He is the man who dominates his competition because he arrives with 100% power and intention. He has eliminated the virus of scarcity and, as a result, is the most unique commodity in the marketplace. He carries no "neediness" or scarcity. He does not chase business; he attracts it.

He dominates his marketplace *without* sacrificing his body, his marriage, his children, or his soul.

THE SALES WAR is the battle between idolatry and God's Will that every salesman faces.

Lies and truth. Scarcity and abundance. Darkness and light. Idolatry and faith. These things are always at war.

The purpose of this book is to give you new weapons to use in this battle so that you can rise from a place of scarcity to a place of power and abundance. It will not be easy. It will not be painless. If you're not ready, close the book. Put it in a seat pocket on your next flight and leave it for another man who is ready.

If you are committed to winning in all areas of your life, including massively growing your business, continue reading. Your commitment will be rewarded.

You will find power in simply turning the next page.

Welcome, brother. I have some weapons for you.

"You shall have no other gods before me."

—Exodus 20:3

WELCOME TO WEAPONS TRAINING

In the following chapters, you will go through a journey and will be given four powerful weapons to equip you to fight The Sales War. Each chapter will give you the basic argument, the story of discovery, and the principles that make it work. You will also find MISSIONS that will give you specific instructions on how you can experience the power of each weapon yourself. Each chapter will also provide a PROTOCOL that will give you a formula to deploy these weapons in daily life for maximum sales impact.

The first three weapons are:

- The Weapon of The Spirit
- The Weapon of The Heart
- The Weapon of The Body

These set the foundation and will give you access to the fourth and final weapon:

- The Weapon of Presence

The weapons give you formulas to completely shift your life and your business if you do the work. Let's face it, most of you who read this book won't do the work. But for the 20% that do, I welcome you to a new possibility: a world where you are dominating your marketplace without sacrificing your body, your marriage, your children, or your soul. Let's go.

CHAPTER 3

THE WEAPON OF
THE SPIRIT

"You do not have, because you do not ask."

James, 4:2

THE WEAPON OF THE SPIRIT

It's not unusual to find yourself alone as a top performer. The drive to deliver results becomes a no-holds-barred race to crush the numbers. We've all felt it. With a vicious commitment to your numbers, it's easy to give yourself an excuse to run over or around anything in your way because "no one will give me a break if the numbers don't come in."

You tell yourself that no one else can understand where you are. No one else can understand the pressure or see the world from this place. In that place of the hyper-focused masculine energy, you put on blinders, and your sole focus is the sales target in front of you. You believe no one understands the pressure. No one is going to help you. You must and WILL do it all yourself. You default to "outwork everyone" mode and live in a fortress of self-imposed solitude. You block out your colleagues, family, and God so that you can focus on taking down the prey. You feel a sense of pride about being the lone warrior, the one who brings home the kill. You actually love being the lone gunslinger who makes it rain when no one else can. In fact, you give yourself a license to make all of your commitments negotiable just as long as you can hit the target and win the game. There is another *lie* that is at the root of the misalignment that leads to so much destruction in our personal and spiritual lives:

"I am alone."

THANK YOU. WILL YOU?

The first-quarter sales numbers were garbage.

All the executives had gone into reaction mode over the team's terrible first-quarter sales numbers. The second quarter was just beginning, and the forecast was not encouraging. After being at the top of the board, I was now at the bottom. It was time to take a dose of humility.

A few days later, I found myself in the office with one of my sales mentors, Pastor Rory Clark. I had known him for thirteen years, and he was who I would always go to when I was in a bind. As we tried to work through how I could hit the massive targets that had been set, he off-handedly said, "You know you can get God in your game, right?"

For a moment, I wasn't sure if he was serious or making a joke about my situation. It was a fact that it would take a literal miracle to hit the revenue targets.

"What do you mean?"

"Hey idiot, you have a relationship with the Sovereign of the Universe, right?"

"Right,"

"Well, why don't you ask Him to get involved in these deals?"

I had never considered this. I had always thought of prayer as something that was ethereal, not directed. I assumed I could only ask for the "big" things. Asking God to help my business seemed too materialistic. I had never considered prayer to be something that could be directed at business results. How would that work? I couldn't wrap my head or heart around it, and I didn't even know how to begin.

I got a text on my phone. It was Susanna asking me when I would be home. I was already late. I hurriedly packed up my gear, told Rory goodbye, and headed home from the office. I would miss dinner again, but I wanted to at least help put my two-and-a-half-year-old daughter Annie Grace to bed.

An hour later, Annie Grace toddled up to me in her pajamas with a copy of "Please, Mr. Panda" in her hands. We had read it the night before, and she loved it.

"Papa, tank you for weeding dis book to me. Will you weed me dis again?" she asked in her sleepy voice as she rubbed her blue eyes.

I felt a wave of gratitude, love, and true joy wash over me. All the background guilt and shame of being late and missing dinner, and not being present with her vanished for the moment.

"Of course I will, baby," I said.

Then a thought entered my mind and hit me hard. I literally felt it. *This is how God feels when we thank him and ask Him for things.*

Annie Grace came and snuggled up to me and opened the book. This revelation had come directly to me *through* my child. She could have asked me to read her a thousand books and for an Arabian pony at that moment, and the answer would have been "YES."

"Thank you. Will you?"

Two days later, at our small church in Dallas, Texas, our pastor delivered a Sunday sermon on the theme of prayer, and he boiled it all down to one simple phrase, "My Father in heaven, I know you can, will you…"

As I heard the words, I made the connection to what Annie Grace had asked.

Thank. Ask.

It was like God was trying to make sure I heard him, but, of course, I was too busy checking emails that night to write any of this down. As I stared at my laptop screen and reviewed the sales calls for the week, a calendar meeting popped up on my screen. "Sales Meeting" was suddenly dropped on my calendar for early the next morning. You've all seen these types of meetings:

- Sales Meeting
- Time: 8:30 AM
- Location: 2nd Floor Conference Room
- Agenda
  - Pipeline review
  - What you're bringing in this week
  - What you're bringing in next week

We all know these meetings are usually a "liar's club." No one really knows what will come in, and no one really means what they say most of the time.

I was frustrated that this had just been dropped on my schedule out of nowhere. These meetings are typically some sales manager's reaction to the pressure being put on him.

I decided I would have my own sales meeting the next day, but it would be one with a far more powerful executive in attendance.

MEETING THE CEO OF THE UNIVERSE

Anytime you can get in front of the Chief Executive Officer of a prospect company as a sales executive, it is always gold. Every business deal accelerates when we get access to power and decision-making. So why don't we call high into the account?

We tell ourselves that the main challenge in the game is getting access to the CEO. They have such limited time. They have huge worries on their minds, and they are surrounded by a bureaucracy that is purposely positioned to insulate them from "people like us." We tell ourselves that there is so much infrastructure surrounding them that we can't possibly get through. We fear rejection, so we don't call them.

We're afraid to call on the CEO because of feelings of fear, unworthiness, or rejection.

We treat God the same way.

But when we finally get up the nerve to just call the CEO of a target prospect, we often find that they are the nicest people, and they appreciate us reaching out to them. We find out that they do have time for us and that often, they instantly accelerate our deal.

I was so triggered that the liar's club sales meeting had been dropped on my calendar last minute that I decided to decline it and schedule my own personal sales meeting.

I decided to have a meeting with the CEO of The Universe.

I set up the agenda in my calendar and sent myself an invite for the next morning:

- Title: Sales Prayer Meeting with The CEO of The Universe
- Time: 8:30 AM
- Location: Ellen's Café, Dallas TX
- Equipment: Journal & Pen
- Agenda:
  ◦ Thank You
  ◦ I know you can, Will You…

The next morning, I arrived on time at Ellen's Café in downtown Dallas.

The waitress showed me to a table, and I sat down and ordered two black coffees.

One coffee for me. One coffee for the CEO.

I took a moment to close my eyes and bow my head to orient myself and be present. I opened my eyes and my journal and labeled it my "WAR MAP."

On the top of the left-hand side, I wrote:

"Sales Prayer Meeting" and the date.

Then below it that I simply wrote:

"My Father in heaven, Thank You for..."

And then I just started writing. I started by thanking him for the deals and the business that had come in (this was a sales meeting after all). As I continued, I found myself thanking him for my family and then all of the other things that came to my heart—many of these things I had not considered before. When I stopped to actually consider all of the things I had to be grateful for, it was impossible to ignore the energetic shift that came with that observation. I wrote until I had exhausted everything I could think of.

I then moved to the top of the next blank page and wrote the following words:

"My Father, I know you can, will you..."

I then started writing out all of the business deals I wanted to close. Every opportunity. Every near-term and long-term target. Everything. I didn't hold anything back. Asking in faith for everything. Once I made my requests about all of the business outcomes, I moved on to all of the other things that were coming up. Requests for my wife and daughters. Requests for my friends and co-workers. Requests for my managers and my CEO. As I wrote, I found that I would discover more things to be thankful for, and I would go back and add to the

"Thank You" section on the previous pages. I continued asking and thanking until I had exhausted all that was on my heart.

I briefly reviewed all of my meeting notes in both the "Thank you" and "Will You" sections.

And with a full heart, signed the meeting notes,

"Your Son, Your Soldier, with Love, Brian Q Davis"

I closed the WAR MAP and said a brief prayer to close the meeting with the CEO.

This exercise causes an energetic shift that is hard to understate. I became aware of how I felt *different*. It took me a few minutes to realize what it was about this feeling that made it feel so strange. I felt powerful. I felt like I was on fire and ready to take on anything. I wasn't worried about the sales numbers anymore. I wasn't worried about *anything*. And then the thought came into my mind that brought it all together.

I am not alone.

Each week as I repeated this process, I found myself constantly moving things from the "WILL YOU" section from the previous week to the "THANK YOU" section for the current week. I saw a pattern begin to emerge. It was consistent. Each week there was more to be thankful for. Each week I would ask my Father for more and more.

Six months after starting this weekly practice, I set all-time sales records and closed the largest deal in our company's history. After having a dismal first half of the year, I ended the year as the top producing salesperson ever. It was not my doing. Huge deals came in that could only have been described as "miraculous." At one point, I won a $1.1M deal with a hospital in Qatar of all places!

There was nothing special that changed about my sales process. I didn't do more cold calls. I didn't have a new product to sell. I didn't have new marketing. The only variable that changed was that I held weekly meetings with the CEO of The Universe and how often I thanked and asked Him.

Now it's your turn to stop operating alone.

"If you then, who are evil, know how to give good gifts to your children, how much more will your Father who is in heaven give good things to those who ask him!" - Matthew 7:11

MISSION:
COFFEE WITH THE CEO OF THE UNIVERSE

The Meeting With The CEO of the Universe is what grounds me in the knowledge that I am not fighting the battle alone. I am never alone, not even in the writing of this book. Indeed, the greatest struggles and resistance during the writing process came when I wasn't asking The CEO for His help.

I have taught this practice through my podcast and in person, and I consistently get messages about the impact that implementing this practice has made on people's lives. Men who had no method to connect with God have used this framework to connect to Him for the first time ever.

Many people feel inclined to run away or turn their backs on a practice like this. Every step towards alignment WILL be met with some resistance, both internal and external. I trust the process. I surrender to the process. When a man takes action and seeks alignment (that's why you're reading this book, by the way), it will often appear bizarre to those out of alignment or not seeking it. Be on the lookout for resistance. It will come, but it won't always look the same. It will show up in yourself, your friends, and your colleagues.

"Why are you ordering two coffees when no one else is here?"

"You can't ask God to help with your sales!"

"God doesn't exist!"

When these voices come, know that it's a confirmation that you are on the right path.

The key to dealing with resistance is surrendering to the process ahead of time. Place the meeting on your calendar and make a commitment to make this meeting happen **no matter what.**

The return on investment for these meetings is massive. These meetings have led directly to millions of dollars in revenue, record sales numbers, and miraculous deals for me and thousands of other men. The meetings have led to revitalized marriages, healed bodies, and transformational spiritual events and experiences. The men who have deployed this weapon in their lives have seen results over and over again. The cost of these meetings is 60 minutes of your time, two cups of coffee, and the humility to trust the process.

The meeting creates an intentional frame for a conversation with the only person in the universe you cannot lie to and is always with you. It simplifies the nature of this conversation, and it removes all the stories we might tell ourselves about our ability to acknowledge God or speak to Him.

When you acknowledge that you have direct access to the CEO of the Universe, everything about your battle plan for hitting the massive sales numbers changes. You no longer say, "It's all on me." Instead, you realize "it's all on Him."

You are no longer alone.

MISSION ACTION PLAN

STEP 1: SCHEDULE THE MEETING

Schedule your first Meeting with the CEO within the next 72 hours. Put the title "Meeting with the CEO of The Universe" on your calendar. The location can be your house, your office, or anywhere, but I find there's value in going somewhere, specifically a restaurant or diner. Get out of your normal space. Where would you go if you were going to meet the CEO of an important prospective client? Bring a journal and a good pen.

STEP 2: RUN THE MEETING

Arrive at your scheduled meeting (on time, please) and get situated at your table—order two coffees (and breakfast if you want it). You may get a strange look for eating alone and ordering two cups of coffee, but that's ok. Put away your phone, be present, and wait for the coffee to arrive. Start the meeting. Title the top of the page in your journal with the following words: "Meeting with The CEO of The Universe"

AGENDA ITEM 1: THANK YOU

Write: "My Father in Heaven, Thank You for..."

Then start writing everything that comes to you that you are thankful for. I often start with all of my business deals or sales that have come in. This is a sales meeting, after all! I then make bullet points of everything else that I can think of. This is the part of the process where you set your feet on a foundation of gratitude.

Here's an example page from a 2019 meeting I had with the CEO straight out of my WAR MAP:

- My Father in Heaven, Thank You for...
  - For the progression on the deals this quarter.
  - For closing the TGMC, BRMC, and PHC deals. Thank you!
  - For my wife Susanna.
  - For my children Annie Grace and Perry.
  - For the healing you are bringing Perry's feet!
  - For giving me the eyes to see the darkness that was attacking this past week.
  - For my brothers.
  - For my coaches Jason and Jennie.
  - For the beauty radiating from my wife.Susanna.
  - For the unexpected bonus money that paid for our vacation.
  - For the awareness to see all of this.
  - For the progress in my body and fitness.
  - For the faith to move forward with hiring an editor for this book.
  - For all that you are showing me.
  - For the growth of my children.
  - For all the deals I see you lining up.
  - For my CEO and all that he has created.
  - For my Brother Jeremy.
  - For my family and getting to see them during the holidays.
  - For protecting my family from the darkness that came after me.
  - For shifting me from fear to my heart last week.
  - For closing the OH Deal!
  - For the scriptures.
  - For your son, Jesus.
  - For His sacrifice.

- For all the revelations.
- For the prayers that the Glitz family sent me last week.
- For the growing friendship with Coach Sam.
- For Brendan King, Deric Keller, Mark MacInerny, Michael Buffington, Jamie Adams, Rustin Kretz, Sam Falsafi, Garrett White....
- For the way the sun looks coming through that window.
- For this coffee.

AGENDA ITEM 2: I KNOW YOU CAN, WILL YOU?

Once you've exhausted everything you're thankful for, leave some space because you're going to remember more things as you move into this next phase. Next, write "My Father in Heaven, I know you can, will You…" and start bulleting all of the things you want to ask for. Remember, you've just been thanking your Father in heaven for all of the things you have been given. This is the step where we ask for what we want, just like my daughter, Annie Grace, did.

The temptation here will be to only ask for things you feel are "worthy of asking God for." You must ignore this feeling. You will likely hear a voice that will tell you that you don't need help or your requests are too small or too big and that you're not worthy enough to ask for them. Acknowledge that resistance and then *ask for everything anyway*. Who are you to put a limit on the CEO of the Universe? Stop thinking small and ASK BIG. Here's an example verbatim from one of my meetings:

- My Father in Heaven, I know you can, will You…
  - Close all the deals I need to hit my targets.

- Please close these deals: BH, AH, PWP, VVH, TGMC, WHC, GMH, PHC, IH, TH, OVHS.
- Move our team beyond the $1M mark this quarter (this happened).
- Set up Q1 to be smashed early.
- Give me the focus to hit my target 60 leads today.
- Give me the flow to create and finish the book and the platform - fill me with your Spirit.
- Close all the deals with no stress.
- Continue to pour into my wife's beautiful energy and spirit.
- Heal the pain in my left shoulder and my lower back.
- Help me hit all targets by the end of the quarter.
- Bless and rise Dan and Rustin and give them power, discern-ment, wisdom, and energy.
- Bless and rise Jamie and give him power, discernment, wisdom, and energy.
- Bless and rise Evelyn and give her power, discernment, wis-dom and energy and set her heart on fire with your love, grace and power.
- Bless and rise Michael B and give him power, discernment, wisdom, and energy. Protect his family and shine your light through them.
- Bless and rise my brother Mark and give him power, discern-ment, wisdom, and energy. Protect and raise his family.
- Bless and rise Coach Sam as the shepherd that he is. Support his heart and shine through him.
- Bless and rise my daughters Annie Grace and Perry so that their light shines for 100 years - Protect them from any corruption or darkness.

- Bless and rise Susanna and let her feel the full power of her beauty and love. Guard her heart.
- Remove any fear from my heart.

When you finish your list, be aware of how you feel. You may notice that a lot of time has passed, and it only seemed like minutes. Once you reach this point, quickly review all of the things you have said "thank you" for and everything you have said "will you" for, close the journal, and say a short prayer of thanksgiving to the CEO for the meeting.

After a single meeting like this, you will feel different than when you started. This foundation of gratitude will support and carry you through the rest of the day and likely your week. You'll often find that the feeling of "being alone" and having to carry the world on your shoulders is gone because you've realized the Truth: *none of us are alone.*

Congrats, you now can feel the presence of the CEO of The Universe in your corner. He has always been there. This power you feel in this first meeting is just the beginning. The real power comes when you have your meetings every week.

When you have your next weekly meeting, follow the same protocol. The only difference is that now you're going to first look at all of the things you asked for in previous meetings. You will almost always find that some of the things you asked for have moved from the "will you" section to the "thank you" section. When I go back to my meeting notes from a few years ago, I find that, in some cases, almost everything I asked for has been granted. Each week, you will find that the momentum builds upon itself.

All things being equal, what salesman do you think will have the advantage in the marketplace? The man who seeks a weekly communion with the ultimate CEO or the one who continues to operate alone with the weight of everything on his shoulders?

There is an unstoppable feeling of power and fellowship that comes when you witness just how powerful and how easy it was to thank and ask and then witness God at work.

WEEKLY PROTOCOL:
COFFEE WITH THE CEO OF THE UNIVERSE

If you take nothing else away from this book, take this practice. Thank You. Will You. I don't care what religion you are. I don't care if you believe in God or you don't. I **dare you** to do this practice for four weeks in a row. I promise you that it will shift your world.

This method has helped the thousands of men who have used it. The evidence is scientific at this point. Many had no idea how to pray or access God. Many had previously turned away from God. Some even hated God. It's easy to hate someone you never talk to. Wherever you are, your Father is waiting. The CEO of the Universe never misses a meeting.

ACTION PLAN

- Schedule weekly "Coffee with The CEO of The Universe" on your calendar for the next four weeks, minimum.
- Allocate a minimum of one hour.
- Bring your WAR MAP/Journal.
- Schedule it at the same place and the same time.
- If you work a traditional business week, early morning or breakfast meetings on Sundays or Mondays are best.

- When you arrive, order two cups of coffee. One for you. One for the CEO.
- Read a verse or two in The Bible. It will ground and orient you.
- Use the following agenda:
  - My Father in Heaven, Thank You for...
  - I know You can, Will You...

NOTE: This is a solid framework. You can customize it to fit your own preferences. This is what I have found works for me. If you want to do "dessert with the CEO" instead of "Coffee with the CEO," that's up to you! Remember though, there's something intentional about bringing GOD specifically into your "business reality." It's the little things, like treating this meeting like it's a true business meeting with a calendar entry in place. This will start to mix these two realities and bring God into your business life. My encouragement would be for you to run it this way and trust the process. It has worked for thousands of others, and it will work for you too.

CHAPTER 4

THE WEAPON OF
THE HEART

"For the moment all discipline seems painful rather than pleasant, but later it yields the peaceful fruit of righteousness to those who have been trained by it."

Hebrews 12:11

THE WEAPON OF THE HEART

It's easy to set yourself up as a savior when you are a high producer. You are the one asked to go to war to kill the competition and make the impossible happen. Like James Bond, you are the elite secret agent who gets the impossible deals done. You operate with impunity. You are willing to sacrifice anything to make the big sales happen.

The truth is that you actually love it when the odds are stacked against you because it increases the adrenaline and cortisol. You love that high. When the odds are against you you can give yourself a License to Kill.

When you finally come home from the mission, road-weary and ragged, you find your wife isn't happy with what you've "done for her." You wonder why she isn't more grateful for your sacrifices. You bring home the bonuses, you buy the nice car and big house, and even then, you find yourself asking, "What is it going to take to make her happy?" You find yourself frustrated and angry when you don't get the respect from your children that "you deserve." Your family wants the big nice expensive things, but they also give you crap for being away on business trips to close the sale. No matter what you do, it's never enough for them!

At least that's the story you are telling yourself. It's the story I was telling myself.

As men, we walk through life with the story that "our family is our responsibility." It's the All-American, family man identity. It's been imprinted in our psyche from early on. We all want to be heroes to our families. This mindset gives us permission to do whatever it takes, whenever we want to "take care of our families."

I used this story to justify the damage I was doing in my pursuit of the Salesman of the Year award. This story gave me permission to abuse my body with sleep deprivation, no exercise, and a poor diet which led to the forty pounds hanging around my waist. I used this story to make it "ok" to leave my wife for weeks at a time during the first years of our marriage as I put the grind in to grow an early-stage startup business seven years prior. I used this story to justify booking eight weeks of travel immediately after the birth of my daughter Perry, leaving my wife at home to deal with clubfoot treatments and braces.

Every day, men like you and me use this "License to Kill" to slowly destroy our marriages, our families, and ourselves.

Operating with this License to Kill would have destroyed everything in my life if not for a single moment of divine clarity and intense pain that changed everything.

WAKE UP, WARRIOR.

I knew *something* was missing. In the six months following the night I exploded at Susanna and Perry for their crying, I started searching. The pain of that night woke me up to the fact that something *must change.* One night in a hotel on another business trip a few weeks later, I saw an advertisement for something called "WarriorBook" that promoted the possibility of a "have it all lifestyle" for married businessmen. I had no idea what it was, but I knew I wanted it. It was from an organization called "Wake Up Warrior" and was led by Coach Garrett J White. I clicked on the ad and bought the "WarriorBook." This book led me down a rabbit hole to find there were thousands of other elite businessmen who were *missing* and *searching* for the same things I was.

The entire movement would be built on two simple principles:

1. Stop lying.
2. Start telling the Truth.

The ultimate expression of their training was a paramilitary-style experiential training event called Warrior Week.

The videos of the training looked like pure punishment, and the lead trainer was a terrifying Persian man with a dark beard and a roaring voice named Coach Sam Falsafi. I knew that the *something* I was missing might be found in the self-selected pain of that event. I had to investigate for the sake of Susanna, Perry, and Annie Grace. I sent in my application for the program and a few days later I was on the phone with Coach Sam.

A QUESTION FOR GOD

August 15, 2017, Laguna Beach, CA - 10:45 AM
WARRIOR WEEK #38

It was the second day of Warrior Week #38. The eighteen men on the hill above the Pacific were all elite high-producers. They were all men with businesses, sales numbers, and families who had been brought to this place looking for the same answers I was. We were all physically and emotionally shattered after the first 24 hours of the Navy SEAL hell week-like beatings. We were all physically, mentally, emotionally, and spiritually exhausted. Some were quiet. Some were crying. Others were bleeding.

We were in the middle of an experience called "The Hand of God," where each man was called to ask God a question. It was my turn to ask the question. My eyes burned from a combination of the hot sun, dust, and the grit that coated everything.

"Ask him your question," said Coach Jesse Ewell, one of the Warrior Week coaches.

I could barely see with the glare of the Pacific Ocean searing my eyes. From 300 feet above the beach, I could see the coastline for miles. Coach Jesse's command hung in the air. Finally, the words croaked out of my dry throat.

"God, what does my family want?"

The shadow of Catalina Island was in the distance. A tiny white sailboat was bobbing just off the coast. I imagined my family was on that boat waiting for me.

A thought formed in my mind.

"My family is not my responsibility."

"What?"

"God doesn't need me."

And then, in a flash, it was all revealed.

I could see all of the destruction I had done to my family, my body, and my soul over the previous five years since I married Susanna. All of the lies I had told myself and others about the work I had been doing "for my family" came rushing at me all at once. It was a high-light reel of pain. All of the nights I had left my wife Susanna alone to face the doctor appointments for Perry. All of the times I could have come home early from a business trip and didn't. All of the time away from my daughters. All of the drinks at the hotel bar. All of the porn in hotels or the bathroom at home. All of the sleep-deprived nights working on sales presentations. All of the extra cocktails in first class on the plane. All of the family dinners not being present and just focused on the next sale.

I could FEEL the loneliness and fear my wife felt when I was gone.

I could FEEL the lack of presence my daughters felt when I was gone or even when I was present.

I could FEEL the damage to my brain from sleep deprivation and inflammation.

I could FEEL the weight of those 40 extra pounds around my waist.

I could FEEL the weight of the secrets my wife did not know.

I could FEEL the GUILT AND SHAME of it all.

License to Kill revoked.

I was free falling into a pit of darkness even as the sun burned down on me.

Then another message came.

"I gave you your family as a DIVINE GIFT…to expand your capacity to hear Me."

The reframe of my family was complete. I saw the truth, and it cut deep. I had been treating my family like a burden that I carried on my back instead of a gift from heaven that I should hold in my hand. But they were more than just a gift; they were messengers from God.

God is communicating to us *through* our families. But we can't hear Him clearly (or at all) when we are busy playing savior to them.

He speaks to us in the words they say, the situations, the circumstances, and the struggles. It was Perry's clubfeet that had been the catalyst for my awakening to the pit I was in but couldn't see. It was the request of my daughter, Annie Grace, asking me to read her a book that had given me the Coffee with the CEO of the Universe process.

Indeed, it was the words of my wife that led me to find the Truth of the Bible six years prior that ultimately led to my salvation. All of these revelations had come *through* my family.

It is only when I let go of the role of savior that I realized the truth and saw my family for what they really were: a gift to expand my capacity to hear God's Voice.

So perhaps our "bitchy wives" aren't so bitchy after all. Perhaps our bratty, spoiled kids are just mirroring our behavior (and showing us what it looks like for God to watch us act like idiots). Perhaps, our families are just asking us to be more than an ego-driven savior.

What if those struggles are just God telling us to listen?

MY FAMILY IS MY FIRE

I fell to my knees on the rocky ground, breaking under the weight of the realization of how I had been operating.

"Your families have all been suffering in silence! Now you will suffer the way your family has," roared Coach Sam.

His intensity was frightening behind the Oakley sunglasses and long dark beard. His black silhouette contrasted with the heat and light from the sun.

"Drop to the ground! Low crawl!"

The entire unit of 18 men dropped to their stomachs into a low army crawl. We had 40-pound rucksacks on our back, filled with sandbags, but the true weight was that of our shame and guilt.

The rocks tore at my ribs as I crawled on my elbows and stomach across the blazing hot hardscrabble ground. My knees and elbows screamed. The path ahead of me and behind me was littered with wounded men who were in agony over their physical situation, but mostly because of the harsh reality of the truth about how they had treated their families.

Jace, a 30-year-old entrepreneur from Kansas, was next to me, and Josh, an orthopedic surgeon from Arizona, was just ahead of me. Josh had dropped his chair, and I feared the repercussions from Coach Sam for losing a piece of equipment. Unlike the way we operated in our families, details mattered here.

I tried to see through the dust to see if there was a finish line. The dust blinded me.

The 40-pound rucksack on my back became my only ally. I found I could shift the weight from side to side to get a little forward momentum. Dust choked my lungs as a large black boot kicked pebbles into my face. We had been crawling for 10 minutes or so. This couldn't go on much longer, right?

Fuck this and fuck these coaches.

"I thought you were some kind of hard man rugby player!" yelled Coach Jesse. "Why don't you just quit, you little fucking bitch!"

Just quit.

Those words started rolling around in my head behind the migraine headache that had erupted in my skull. Each crawl scratched new gouges in elbows and knees. It felt like someone was stabbing me over and over again between my ribs. The fabric of my black tactical pants gave way and started to rip, leaving my skin exposed to the sandpaper ground. It was white-hot pain.

With nothing left, I laid my forehead down in the dust and tried to find my breath.

"Just quit."

I had a flash vision of Roman soldiers kicking and spitting on a bloodied and abused man. His skinned knees and shredded hands collided with the rocky path as he struggled under the weight of a massive wooden beam. Humiliation. Agony.

What got Jesus through it?

"His love for you. Go there."

My focus had only been on the pain. As my forehead pressed into the dirt in front of me, an image of my wife and daughters broke through the pain in my head. They were in pain. The chaos around me faded.

I felt a shift start to happen. The torture in my head began to give way to power rising from my heart. I could literally feel the energy shift from the front of my head to my chest. The only way to free my family from the pain was to get to the end of the path. I moved from my head to my heart.

"Perry." One crawl forward.

"Annie Grace." Another crawl.

"Susanna." Another crawl.

A blind fury consumed me. I was fighting to get to my family. They were giving me the power to overcome the pain. I spit dust.

"Perry! Annie Grace! Susanna!"

Each of their names manifested power. With each name, I took one crawl forward. With each crawl, pain seared their names into my heart. This is what it is to suffer in love. This is how my family would feel if I continued sedating myself with business and ego. This was God speaking to me through my family. This was my family broadcasting God's message to me.

The Divine Gift of my family was CHANGING ME.

Such love. Such power. Such fury. Such fire. As the pain in my body increased, so did my power and capacity. The pain became more bearable every time I spoke their name. This love and power were impossible without them. This transformation was impossible without them.

Another flash vision of Christ and His peaceful fury and submission to save us all on that hill. We were the family HE was suffering for on that rock.

I had stopped looking for the finish line and just *went*. Over and over, their names flowed from my heart to my voice. I could hear men around me doing the same. The names of sons, daughters, and wives filled the dry air. The shift was happening on that hill. Men were finding the fire required to make it through, this not in their heads, but through the GIFT OF THEIR FAMILIES, and it came from their hearts.

Moments later, I found myself across the finish line with my face in the dirt, gasping for breath next to my brother, Josh.

I was exhausted. I was bleeding. My heart was full of the fire of my family, but just thirty minutes later, I would find myself in darkness again.

A GIFT OF TIME

August 15, 2017, Laguna Beach, CA - 3:32 PM
WARRIOR WEEK #38

The only light I could see was coming in around the edges of the darkness in front of my eyes.

It was like a corona around an eclipse.

The black Mercedes Sprinter van shook as it thundered down the highway to its next destination. The eighteen men of Warrior Week 38 sat crowded together in the backs of the van. Each of us was blind-folded and had a black hood over our heads. No man had the energy to resist the process. All that was left was surrender.

Each man was imprisoned in that darkness, forced to be present with only his thoughts about his life.

The vans came to a halt, and an intense silence lingered in the air. No one spoke. No one moved. The sound of the van doors opening seemed louder than usual. Something about the metal sliding past metal was frightening.

"Get out. No talking." growled Coach Jesse.

By this point, we all knew the drill. We kept our blindfolds and hoods on, each man instinctively reaching out to find the shoulder of the man next to him. We filed out and found our way to a shoulder-to-shoulder position.

The air was cooler here. It was quiet.

It was a stark contrast to the horror of the crawl on the hill just an hour before.

"Take off your blindfolds," said Coach Jesse.

The light was intense after that much darkness.

"Follow us," said Coach Sam.

Coach Sam walked up the lush green grassy hill off to our left. There was a silhouette of an angel that stood at the top of the hill.

This particular angel stood watch over the graves of hundreds of dead children.

The angel had the face of a little girl. Her face looked up to heaven. Her hands were outstretched with her palms facing up as if she was prepared to catch something. Her hair was short and wavy. She reminded me of my daughter, Perry. The plaque at her feet read, "The Angel of Hope."

We were ordered to stand in a semi-circle, facing the angel. The larger copper statue marked the gateway of the children's section of this massive graveyard. At the base of the statue were the words,

"Our Children, Loved, Missed, and Remembered," etched into the granite base.

"Take off your boots."

Each man took off his boots and placed them in tight order around the base of the statue.

"This way," said Coach Sam.

Each man followed the one before him, single file, walking barefoot across the grass. I glanced behind me and saw one man staying behind.

Coach Jesse, who had been a ferociously intimidating figure up until this point, was still at the statue, kneeling in prayer.

We walked up the hill among hundreds of headstones. Coach Sam ordered us to sit down in another semicircle on a set of pre-arranged chairs. Everyone was still. The only sound was the wind.

There was a large headstone in front of us, but something was different about it. There were three names on it. They all had the same last name. Each name had a different birthdate on it but they all had one thing in common.

The death date.

These three children had all been taken at once, on the same day.

Twenty men sat in absolute stillness as the gravity of the story of this unknown family washed over us.

There is nothing like considering death to make you consider life. Coach Sam ordered us to stand up and walk through the graves. "There is a message waiting for you here. Go."

I walked up the hill to the right to find a place to pray. I didn't have far to go to hear a call. I looked down and saw musical notes etched in one of the head-stones. I knelt in front of the black marble marker, journal in hand.

The sun was bright and warm and glimmered through the trees. There was just stillness.

Olivia Anne Overturf had lived 16 months and 16 days. Her headstone lay flush with the lush grass in the children's section of the El Toro Memorial Park in Lake Forest, California. It read:

Olivia Anne Overturf,

March 8, 2010 - July 23, 2011

"Beautiful memories silently kept of a baby
we love and will never forget."

I took out my journal and started writing.

"I don't know how long I will have them, or they will have me.

There are children dying and parents suffering every day.
Do I act in honor with my time so that I could look any of them in the face?

Time is a gift.

Honor it."

These words materialized on the page in my journal in front of me as I stared at the headstone.

I felt the weight of the sadness of her parents. I felt the weight of the love they had for her.

Tears streamed down my face.

There was a tap on my shoulder. It was Coach Jesse.

"Let's go, brother. It's time for the next evolution," he said.

What was about to happen next would change my life, and shortly you too will have an opportunity to change yours. But first, let's explore the lessons behind this shift.

PRINCIPLES: THE WEAPON OF THE HEART

PRINCIPLE #1: YOUR FAMILY IS NOT YOUR RESPONSIBILITY. GOD DOESN'T NEED YOU. YOUR FAMILY IS A DIVINE GIFT THAT EXPANDS YOUR CAPACITY TO HEAR HIM.

The idea that our families are burdens (aka "responsibilities") is built into the American subconscious.

We say things like "the ole' ball and chain," which literally suggests we are imprisoned by our families. The idea that our family somehow restricts our freedom is the baseline story that most men and society at large tell themselves.

Our wives and children are viewed as a tightening tourniquet on our capacity. They limit our time. They require attention. They require resources and money. They limit our production.

Resentment towards them starts to build when these requirements inevitably collide with the demands of our sales numbers and production targets.

"How can I possibly hit my numbers when my wife wants me home at 5:30 in the afternoon?"

"How can I get all my calls in when my two-year-old is waking up at 5:00 AM?"

"How can I catch up and be prepared for next week when my family takes up all my time on the weekend?"

"Doesn't my wife know that I've got TO SELL to pay the bills?"

"All these kids do is spend money. They don't appreciate shit."

Sound familiar? This is an especially dangerous trap for new fathers.

Data from a 2015 study suggest that the divorce rate within the sales industry is 38.7%, ranking among the top 10 industries with the highest divorce rates.[2] That is a lot of chaos and destruction, considering there are over 4.5 million business-to-business salespeople in the US. When I dug deeper into the research and looked at the top reasons why people get divorced, it was even more revealing.

Top Reasons for Divorce[3]:

1. Lack of communication
2. Infidelity
3. Inability to resolve conflict
4. Drifting apart
5. Financial Issues
6. Married for the wrong reasons
7. Different priorities
8. Lack of freedom
9. Abuse

These are symptoms of one core thing: misalignment. This mis-alignment slowly builds for years and creates a spiritual weight that we literally start to "carry" around. We bring this energetic drag of unacknowledged guilt and shame into our sales

---

2. American Community Survey, 2015 https://flowingdata.com/2017/07/25/divorce-and-occupation

3. https://www.divorcenet.com/resources/common-reasons-marriages-end.html

presentations, our prospecting, and our negotiating. In order to avoid the pain, we typically refuse to look at it and sedate so we don't have to feel it. We pull our "License to Kill" whenever we need to give ourselves permission to skip the family meal, look at porn, miss our kids' sports games, have the extra drink, skip date nights, or text the woman we just met at the bar at the conference.

Underneath the weight of all this guilt, shame, and sedation, God's voice grows increasingly distant. Misalignment in marriage and family life begins when it is viewed from the frame of *restriction* instead of *expansion.* The idea that marriage and family restrict freedom is *the inverse of the Truth.*

Thankfully, God never stops broadcasting. When you are completely out of alignment, God will use your family to speak to you. Perhaps you've experienced this. What is your family "saying" to you now?

In every situation with your family, you can ask, "What is God trying to tell me?" and then check what the Word says.

Their words matter. The stress that's created by our families is no longer a burden but an aligning force. When we pay attention, we start to seek to be present with them, not out of compulsion but out of desire. We feel God's presence every moment we spend with them. We come to KNOW that revelations and guidance will come through them.

PRINCIPLE #2: MY FAMILY IS MY FIRE.

When we listen to our families this way, God allows us to access a level of fire and fury that we can channel into our production in massive ways. We can go harder and further than our competition. We are more creative in building solutions. We are more powerful in our presentations and negotiations. Without any baggage of shame and guilt about how we are treating our families, we walk taller. We look better. Our energy is founded in love, not scarcity. The certainty that comes from knowing that your kingdom is not burning down gives you a new kind of fire: the fire of your family.

You are not working *for* your family. You are channeling power *from* your family.

I had nothing left on that crawl on the hill. When I turned my heart to my family, I accessed a type of fire that would have been unavailable without them.

I no longer chase down sales numbers, commissions, and the big bonus "for my family." I win because I bring the power of my family and my heart into the marketplace. I would never want to compete as a single man versus a man who is drawing on the power of his family. It wouldn't be a contest. Fortunately, for the single men that read this, most married men are not willing to do the work to establish this channel of power.

This gift of FIRE is available to you. When a man accesses the power of his family through his heart, it immediately increases his capacity in ALL domains. Your workouts become more intense (more on that in The Weapon Of The Body), your connection to God expands, your connection with your children grows, and friendship and intimacy with your wife increase (yes...more sex...lots more).

But, you must be willing to let go of your ego-driven story of being the savior of your family. You must reframe your family, viewing them no longer as a "responsibility" but a "Divine Gift." Maintaining this perspective requires a daily commitment, and there is a simple process to do this. But before we go there, we have to go to someplace dark to find the fire...just like I did.

To access this kind of power and fire, you must pay a price. Do not take the next step in this journey lightly.

Gather yourself and trust the process.

This next part will hurt.

MISSION: THE LAST LETTER

The next evolution at Warrior Week would expose everything for me about my orientation to my family. It was painful and revealing and would be the single moment that would encapsulate this entire experience. It was also the place that would lock in the fire of my family.

Your time with your family is finite. Somewhere, someplace, there is a universal clock and the timer is counting down. It's waiting for you to feel this reality.

Your next mission is to write a letter. And just like your life, you will have limited time to do it.

You will need the following resources for this assignment:

- Your journal
- A pen
- A timer

Now ask this question: What if you only had *fifteen minutes* to live from this very moment?

What would you say to your wife, your children, or others?

You are going to find the answers to these questions NOW. Do not take this mission lightly, and do not rob yourself of this gift. Trust the process.

MISSION ACTION PLAN

Assume that wherever you are, on a flight, in a taxi, or sitting in your office, that you only have fifteen minutes to live. You are somehow aware that the flight is going to crash, the taxi will be hit by a drunk driver, or that you are going to have a massive heart attack or brain aneurysm and die instantly.

You cannot call or text anyone.

The only thing you can do is leave a letter.

STEP 1: Grab your journal and pen.

STEP 2: Set your timer for fifteen minutes.

STEP 3: Start the timer, turn the clock so you can't see it and begin writing your Last Letter to your family.

Once the timer goes off, <u>drop your pen right where it is</u>.

Don't try to write another word. Don't try to finish the sentence.

Set another ten-minute timer and spend this time reviewing and journaling what you observe about your letter. Observe what you feel and write it down in your journal.

Your family is so much more than just your wife and children. They are messengers, and this is a window for them to deliver a Divine message to you.

Set up your timer for 15 minutes. Do not watch the clock.

Ready?

Three, two, one...off you go.

RETURN AND REPORT

Welcome back. Before we get started, I wanted to share my own "Last Letter" from that day in the cemetery:

My Dearest Susanna, Annie Grace & Perry Elizabeth -

This is my last message to you while I am here on earth, and oh how I will miss you so.

Susanna, you are the greatest friend, partner, lover, wife, and Queen mother that I could ever hope for.

Annie Grace, you were my first baby and introduced me to what being a father feels like.

Perry Elizabeth, you were the one who showed me what strength looks like.

I know all of you know I love you, but I don't think you all know how much I love you.

Why?

Because you showed me what it is to be a person - to be a man - to be a version of me that I never knew existed.

In fact, it never existed until each of you.

I should have shown you more. I should have said to hell with all the things that took me away from you - when I know the only thing you ever really wanted from me was "me."

I'm sorry I didn't give more - of myself. I am sorry I didn't give ALL OF MYSELF.

And I never knew Him until I met you, my dearest love. What greater gift could you have given me than the introduction to Salvation?

What an incredible woman you are. Our children are safe with you.

You are my dearest love - I wish I would have treasured you more. You are the greatest gift God put in my life. Please know I loved you from the first minute to the last.

Please live life for yourself & our girls after I am gone. Don't hold back. I always wanted to see the Butterfly unfurled! I'm sorry I didn't do more. I'll see you in heaven my love. I am yours. Always.

Annie Grace - my best buddy, my light and laughter. I love you so much. Please follow your mama. You can't go wrong. Learn about and follow Christ. You are my Spartan Princess. Rise to be a Queen my love.

*Dear sweet Perry, you sho_*

(END LETTER)

That last line. That's the part that hurts. In the letter, Perry, my youngest daughter, didn't get the rest of her message. If this was truly my last letter, she would spend her whole life wondering what I was going to say to her.

And therein lies the gift from my daughter Perry. Once again, God was speaking through my family in the gift of an unfinished sentence. The pain that came with that unfinished sentence was the source of FIRE that would bring URGENCY to the change that must happen. NOW.

What was your unfinished sentence?

The unfinished sentences in your letter and the feeling they create is A GIFT. Yes, it hurts, but this is the path, The Weapon Of The Heart.

PROTOCOL: DAILY NOTES OF POWER

Now that you know where The Weapon of The Heart is, how can you put it into practice? In the following protocol, you will find a very simple set of actions that, if deployed consistently, will open a gateway for you over the next ninety days. It all starts with a DAILY orientation of your heart to your family.

Every day for the next ninety days, you will create a written note each morning to each member of your immediate family.

The framework for each written note is as follows:

Dear ( ),
"I honor you because…
I love you because….
I appreciate you because…"

Select one or more of these statements to frame your note.

During the act of writing the note, the orientation of your heart will shift. One of the most important things to know is that you are doing this for YOU, not them. It is in the act of creating each note that the orientation of the heart shifts. It is literally inside the twenty to thirty seconds of writing those notes where the shift happens.

You will write these notes every day regardless of circumstance.

If you and your wife are fighting, you write the note. If you and your children are fighting, you write the note.

If you are leaving your family for a few days, you write notes ahead of time and pre-stage them, so they are delivered each day. Do this by putting them into an envelope designated for each day and leave them to be opened while you are gone.

Each day, take a picture of each note. Create a folder on your phone or computer and save all of these pictures in that special place so you can easily access them later.

If you have small children, who can't read, draw a picture that connects with the emotion of the message. Your little ones will understand them. You don't have to be an artist, but I found that the act of creating a drawing helps cement the intention for me while making it accessible to even small children.

These notes are written and given with NO EXPECTATION. Don't expect a response. Depending on your current relationships and your past behavior, your family may initially reject your notes. It doesn't matter if they love them or hate them, you write them. The end.

Additional tips:

1. Do your notes/drawings first thing in the morning. Literally, make it the first thing you do when you wake up. Do not look at social media, your email, news, or anything else. Wake up, do your notes. I like to do them while having coffee.

2. Tape your notes somewhere visible. I literally covered our refrigerator with notes over a two to three-month period. There is something about the visual manifestation of consistency that creates a compounding effect. Your wife sees your consistency, your children see it, but most importantly, you see it. Eventually, my wife took them off the refrigerator because it needed cleaning. I saw it as a new blank canvas. My daughter, Annie Grace, took several hundred of her notes and posted them on the walls in her room. Some have been there for years. When

I ask her about them, she can tell me what every one of them means.

3. At the end of every month or every quarter, create a book out of the pictures that you took and give it as a gift to your family members. This can be easily done with various apps. I personally use an app called "Chatbooks." I title my books "The Power I See In …. (insert name)" and create a new volume every quarter. It's hard not to consider how our children will value these books in the future. I imagine my daughters looking back on these books when they are faced with future challenges and gaining power from witnessing the power I see in them.

CONCLUSION

As long as you are "carrying" your family as a burden, you will always have an energetic drag that will limit your potential and production. You were not born to be a savior. That job belongs to only one Man. You were born to be a leader. God put people in your life to love so that you can experience what it's like for Him to love you. He gave you these people so that you can experience what it means to orient your heart and build from that place of love.

Everything becomes easier when the fire of your family fuels you. Everything accelerates when you do the work, orient your heart, and bring it to the marketplace. You will be able to do the hard things, the things that must be done, because of your greater capacity. You'll become more creative. You'll be more present. You'll become more powerful in every area, including your marketplace and sales.

The Weapon of The Heart is more powerful than anything in your head.

Draw the weapon.

CHAPTER 5

THE WEAPON OF
THE BODY

"So I do not run aimlessly; I do not box as one beating the air. But I discipline my body and keep it under control, lest after preaching to others I myself should be disqualified."

1 Corinthians 9:26–27

THE WEAPON OF THE BODY

The life of a sales executive is brutal on the body. The body is the first thing that becomes negotiable as we chase down the big numbers. The physical sedations of men working in sales are many and often creep into patterns and behaviors over the years. Perhaps you're experiencing some of this now?

- **Sleep deprivation** – Always staying up late to over-prepare or give up sleep to do proposals or RFPs. It gets even more intense with small children.

- **Lack of exercise** – With no plan, you skip the hotel gym and allow the disruption of constant travel to give you the "out," even when you are home.

- **Inconsistent diet and unhealthy food** – You eat whatever comes with First Class on the flight, and you eat the garbage at the airports. You eat fancy meals with the clients and never say no to dessert.

- **Alcohol** – Of course you'll have drinks with the client and then more drinks at the airport bar and then more on the flight because, "Why not? I've put in the work."

- **Pornography** – There's nothing like an empty hotel room to sedate in. No interruptions. High-speed bandwidth. Unlimited variation and quantity. At home, you hide from your wife in the bathroom or the shower like a teenager.

- **Infidelity** – Ultimate destruction comes when you are weakened by exhaustion and alcohol, and temptation comes in the form of late-night drinks in the hotel room with a colleague or the person you met at the conference or trade show. You hope no one notices, but we've all seen it. The cycle of lies, guilt, shame, hiding, and sedation begins again.

Have you ever noticed how people just seem to "swell" over time? It's more than just "age-related" weight gain or bad habits. It's the spiritual weight and inflammation of the guilt and shame that continues to compound on itself over the years. Perhaps this is you? It was me. I sedated myself with everything you see above, with the exception of infidelity, but the night I looked in the mirror after yelling at Susanna and Perry, I saw a clear and dark vision of divorce in my future if my behavior didn't change.

My body failed me on that crawl on the hill during Warrior Week. I was exposed. I had been humbled by the reality that I *was not* strong anymore. I lived with constant background anxiety about my physical appearance. I had lost the once strong and fit physique I built playing 17 years of rugby. I was at the mercy of my body's urges. Food. Sugar. Porn. Alcohol. Whatever would take the edge off of a long day of travel and the stress of chasing the idol. I was constantly hiding my pear-shaped dad-bod by always wearing black shirts and oversized suit coats.

It had literally been years since I'd intentionally trained my body with any level of intensity. The last time I'd tried to get in shape had been in the months leading up to my honeymoon. It was totally out of ego. I had lost my "why" to train after retiring from rugby. I realized I had gone years without taking my shirt off during the summer.

I also had an unspoken worry about potential brain damage. My primary sedation was sleep deprivation. I still have trouble recalling periods of time during my oldest daughter's first year without pictures. There was a period where I was averaging three hours of sleep per night as I crushed through RFP docs and over-prepared for every presentation in pursuit of Salesman of The Year. I was compensating for my lack of certainty.

The crawl on the hill made me realize that something had to change. My body was the biggest initial roadblock. If I couldn't face the truth of where I was in my physical being, I wouldn't be able to face the truth anywhere else. The inflammation in my physical being was a manifestation of my spiritual reality.

Things will start to shift when you view your body as a weapon that is critical to your performance in sales and life.

LOG P.T.

Few things will humble a man faster than holding a weight overhead for an extended period of time.

Log Physical Training or "Log P.T." is used to humble Navy Seal applicants in the legendary "BUDS" training. It's a powerful device that SEAL instructors use to expose weakness within men and teams while building unity under stress.

Log P.T. typically consists of a group of eight to ten men working with a 250 to 300-pound log and going through a set of sequences of picking it up, putting it down, lifting it, carrying it, and any number of other monotonous and torturous movements.

If you're not familiar with this type of training, look it up, and you'll see what I'm talking about. As I headed into Warrior Week, I knew Log P.T. would be part of the experience. I was scared. I had played rugby for years, but I had been out of the game for seven years. I decided there was no way I was going to be the weak link during the training.

I had only five weeks until I'd be entering Warrior Week, and I had to figure out a way to simulate the Log P.T. evolution. I rewatched some of the Log P.T. videos and actually timed the overhead hold. It typically lasted five to seven minutes. I then did the math to figure out that assuming a log was three hundred pounds and that log had an average of ten men on it, that the average load would be approximately 30 pounds. Of course, in reality, this is far from accurate as the actual load is entirely a factor of the coordination, teamwork, endurance, and to some extent, the height of each man. This also doesn't take into account the duration of the training and when the instructor might deploy a static hold of the log.

After doing the math, I had figured out a drill I could do to train (or so I thought).

I had a rusty 35pound dumbbell, and all I had to do was hold it over my head for seven minutes. This was my formula for "Simulated log P.T." Easy!

Right?

On my first attempt, I set a timer for seven minutes and picked up the weight.

Just three minutes later, sweating and shaking, I was crushed.

All I could think about during the hold was, "how much longer?"

Every time I looked at the timer, time slowed down, and I got weaker.

I was weak.

In the days that followed, I continued to practice the Simulated Log P.T. Instead of a timer, I substituted a set of songs that would line up with the length of the desired duration. I knew I needed something to distract me from that timer. The two songs I chose were "Undercover" by Jeremy Finlay, which, incidentally, became the opening music for The Sales Warrior Podcast a year later, and "Never Stop" by Jung Youth (who I later became friends with and had as a guest on my podcast). The two songs together lasted exactly seven minutes.

I found that by focusing on the music, not the timer, I increased my capacity by a minute or so. But, I still couldn't make it beyond the first four minutes.

Then one morning, just after writing my notes of love, honor, and gratitude to my girls, I asked myself the question: "What if I didn't focus on the music but focused on my wife and daughters?"

What if I framed the effort of holding this weight overhead and made it a fight for my family?

I took out my phone and pulled up a picture of my family to look at, turned on the playlist, and picked up the dumbbell.

I could feel a difference in the effort. The intention was different. I was no longer doing the workout out of fear of being weak. I was no longer focused on how long I would do it. I was no longer focused on the timer. I was focused on fighting for my family.

By minute three, sweat was pouring down my face. By minute four, the fire in my shoulders was intense. The pain increased. Every time I heard a voice say, "Drop the weight," I would focus on the picture of my family and counter it with the question, "Will you drop them?"

This loop starts in the mind.

"Quit"

"Don't quit."

"Quit"

"Never. I won't quit on them."

There was power in resisting that voice.

My arms caved at six minutes. I was drenched in sweat but felt on fire.

By simply orienting my focus towards my family, I increased my power and endurance by 30%.

I was left feeling the deep love *of* and *for* my family.

This shift in intention showed me the power that was available when I chose to fight with my heart instead of my head.

I was still out of shape. I was still carrying around those 40 pounds. But, I was able to carry these six minutes of fire into the rest of my day. I brought it to work, to all of my sales calls and conversations. The energy I had was more powerful. It was a *different* energy.

Suddenly, I had a renewed awareness of my body. There was power there, and I could access it.

Over the next year, this awareness would set the foundation for another set of practices. This discovery would transform my body from a pear-shaped sales guy into a weapon, but it would require a new level of warfare.

In the previous chapter, The Weapon of The Heart, I described how turning inward and drawing strength and fire from my family during the crawl on the hill was the only thing that got me through it. I wanted to make sure I never ever forgot this, so I brought it into my workouts as a practice following the crawl on the hill. I had to reprogram the way I thought about my body.

All of my years of rugby training had taught me that there was only one way to work out: according to a schedule. My schedule was loosely based on a structure that assumed there was a game on the weekends. Monday was leg day. Wednesday and Friday were upper body or power days. Tuesday and Thursday were rugby training days. Saturday was game day, and Sunday was rest day (or "recover from a hangover day"). All of this structure and rigor works well when you're playing rugby or training for weekend competitions. But, when I found myself "retired" from rugby after moving away from California in 2010, I lost all of that structure, connection, and commitment.

Then I had a coach introduce me to the simplest form of a daily war:

Sweat every day.

The end.

The operative part of the formula is "every day."

I didn't have a gym membership at the time. All of my traveling and overworking had created a story, one that said, "I won't be home long enough to really use it." But I was committed and accountable to my coach, so I forced myself to find some way to get a workout in. I found an app that provided a set of bodyweight exercises that I could do anywhere (including any hotel room) and started committing to the formula. "Sweat every day."

After just four weeks, I lost ten pounds.

Since that time, I've gone on to lose a total of 40 pounds and, at 45, I am more fit than I've ever been. Fitness went from something I did to something I am. But it started with getting clear about my "why."

I no longer move my body "to get in shape." I move to **get in power.** But the power is no longer just physical power. It's spiritual. Here's my formula that helped transform an out-of-shape "businessman" with a dad bod gut into an athlete that would put my 30-year-old self to shame.

In the following section, I'm going to give you some of the basic principles and practices that will transform the way your body operates (and looks!).

PRINCIPLES: THE WEAPON THE BODY

PRINCIPLE #1: ELIMINATE DECISIONS

When you're trying to build physical activity into who you are, decision-making will kill your momentum. Here are some of the most common momentum-killing decisions:

- What workout do I do?
- What days do I work out?
- What if I miss a workout?
- Did I get enough rest?
- What if I'm still sore?
- What if the gym is closed?
- What if I can't find a gym at the hotel?
- What if I forgot my gym clothes?

All of these questions create decision fatigue (which is a real thing). When you make things simple, you won't have the extra weight of all these decisions. Without those barriers, you become consistent. And here is the secret: consistency with little things delivers bigger results faster than massive, inconsistent efforts. This is true of workouts and pretty much everything else in life. So let's start by eliminating some of those decisions for you right here, right now.

PRINCIPLE #2: EVERY DAY IS TRAINING DAY

YOUR NEW WORKOUT SCHEDULE: EVERY DAY (Ideally first thing in the morning)

It's easier to work out every day than on certain days. What counts as a workout? Anything that breaks a sweat. A five-mile run? Yes. A one-minute plank? Yes. The commitment is to put yourself in POWER every day. With this frame, every day you don't sweat is a day where you operate with less power than you could have. Everything slows down.

Conversely, every time you meet your commitment to sweat every day, you are making a deposit in your own bank of personal integrity and certainty. Over time, you will be shocked by what you can achieve and how your body will transform. Be sure to take pictures of yourself.

PRINCIPLE #3: YOU ARE THE GYM

WORKOUT ROUTINE: BODYWEIGHT EXERCISES – THE NO EXCUSES WORKOUT SYSTEM

Traveling always screwed up my workout schedule. The unpredictable nature of business travel can lead to all sorts of bad decisions in terms of how we eat, sleep, and move. It also gives us an easy set of excuses to use on the road:

- "They don't have the equipment I like at the hotel gym."
- "I don't have time before the meeting this morning."
- "I don't know where to run around here."
- "I'm too tired."
- "I'll just wait until I get home to work out."

These same excuses ruled my mindset for years. When every day became training day, I was required to find a solution. I needed a formula so I could work out every day, anywhere, anytime, with zero resources or equipment. I found the answer in a little app that changed everything for me.

PRO TIP: BODYWEIGHT WORKOUT APPS

I don't know how I found it, but it arrived just in time. The Adidas Runtastic Results app has an extensive library of bodyweight exercise routines that range from the short and easy to the absolutely grueling (more on that in a minute). There are workouts that can be done in two to three minutes and others that can take over an hour. The point is that there was no longer an excuse for not having enough time or not having the right equipment. The app provides workouts that will help you break a sweat every time. All you need is a space the size of a beach towel or yoga mat. The app gamifies the experience by recording your time as you progress through the workout so that the next time you perform that workout, you now have a record to beat. It becomes a game of "you vs. you." Every day.

When I removed all of the excuses, the only barrier left was myself. But once I started feeling the power of making the CHOICE to put myself in power every day, it was addictive. And then changes started happening. The weight started to fall off. Interest in sedations like food, porn, alcohol, and sugar started to fade. I started to build a new foundation. I adopted habits that served me instead of ones that sedated me. You can too. Eliminate decisions. Eliminate excuses. Forget getting in shape. GET IN POWER.

PRINCIPLE #4: THE BURPEE IS A WEAPON

There is nothing that will shift your energetic state faster than a round of chest-to-ground burpees. I see it as embodied prayer. The end.

PRINCIPLE #5: YOUR FAMILY IS YOUR FIRE

As I would go into these workouts, I would visualize my wife and two daughters. I would create a mental picture of each of them and then "circle" them with five reps. I used this leverage to power through more and more reps. I might quit on myself, but I would never quit on them. I would literally see their faces, circle them with five reps, and repeat. This daily practice of "circling my family" served to orient my heart towards them on a daily basis. It serves as a daily reminder to view them for what they are: a divine gift and access point to divine fire.

In the following section, you're going to be given two missions. They are not going to be comfortable, and they will hurt, but the objective is to wake you up to a new mindset about what your body is and learn how it can be used to access power to fight your way out of any darkness you may face.

MISSION 1: "SIMULATED" LOG P.T.

On this mission, you're going to learn the following:

1. How quickly and easily you can break a sweat and shift your energetic state

2. How you can access a new level of presence and awareness in your body (this will be valuable in the next chapter - The Weapon of Presence)

3. How you can access a greater power by orienting your heart towards your family

As previously mentioned, this simple practice was the gateway. It woke up my sedated, out-of-shape body and opened up a new level of awareness and power. You can do this too, and it will only take a few minutes.

MISSION ACTION PLAN

What you'll need:

1. 30-35 pounds of weight. This can be a dumbbell, sandbag, or any object you can easily (safely) hold over your head.
2. A quiet place where you can be alone. This is not an activity you want to do in the middle of a crowded gym. You must be alone and uninterrupted.
3. A timer or your phone.
4. A picture of your family.

Evolution 1: Simulated LOG P.T. - "In your head" version

In this round, we're going to play the simplest form of the game.

- Get your weight. Get your timer and make sure you are in a quiet place where you will not be interrupted. Do not use music. Do this evolution in silence.
- Place the timer where you can see it.
- Start the timer and lift the weight over your head.
- Continue to watch the timer. Hold the weight until failure.
- If you lower the weight below the top of your head, the round is over.
- Stop your timer and record how long you held the weight.

   3, 2, 1...off you go!

Round 1: Return and Report

Congratulations. You broke a sweat today.

You are probably also beating yourself up about how few minutes you were able to hold the weight. There's no doubt that this simple experience can bring massive awareness to your physical being. Before you let too much guilt and shame set it, let's move on to round two and play a more powerful game.

Evolution 2: Simulated LOG P.T. - "From Your Heart" Version

In this round, you will repeat the same experience, but this time with two different elements.

1. You will start the timer but put it in a place where **you cannot** see it.

2. You will set the frame in your mind that you are "holding your family" above you and must keep them (i.e., the weight) up longer than your previous time.

3. Instead of focusing on the timer, you will focus on a picture of your family.

4. If you'd like, you can use music during this round.

5. Start your music. Start your timer and turn it away. Set your picture where you can see it.

6. Lift the weight over your head and **go to war** for your family.

3, 2, 1...off you go!

Note: If you'd like access to my original Simulated Log PT playlist, go to www.thesaleswar.com/weapons

Round 2: Return and Report

What did you notice, and what was your result? You likely fell into one of the following outcomes:

- I felt stronger and beat my previous time.
- I felt stronger, but I still fell short of my previous time.
- I felt weaker and fell short of my previous time.

Regardless of the outcome, comparing round one with round two has helped you learn something about yourself.

PROTOCOL:

Sweat every day for thirty days. For some of you, this may be a radical change. For others, if this is already your practice, you are going to add a new level of intensity and spiritual focus to your workouts. What happens if you miss a day? Get back on the horse and go again. No shame. No guilt. Just new choices. The purpose is to grow your certainty by growing your integrity with yourself.

ADVANCED MISSION: SPIRITUAL WARFARE PROTOCOL

I soon discovered that this path not only held the keys to building physical power, but also opened the door to another power I never expected.

As I progressed in using these daily bodyweight workouts over the next six months, I started looking for ways to further streamline my mornings.

I set a target to read the entire Bible in one year, but I found it was very difficult to stay caught up on the readings. In order to save time, make progress, and hit my target, I switched from reading the Bible every day to listening to an audio recording of it every day during my workouts. I replaced my normal workout playlist, Rage Against The Machine and Rocky soundtracks, with daily recordings of Scripture.

It wasn't long before I noticed something happening. There is something about intentionally putting the body under stress for a long enough period of time that opens the heart. I discovered that about the two-thirds mark in most of the workouts, I would get massive downloads and revelations from the Divine. Sometimes they would bring me to my knees in tears during the session.

When the elements of audible Scripture, family visualization, and intense workouts unified, they became something else entirely.

This is called The Spiritual Warfare Protocol.

This singular practice integrates the three practices of spirit, heart, and body and creates something more than just a workout: it is a weapon against the darkness.

THE BEST DEFENSE AGAINST THE DARKNESS IS A GOOD OFFENSE

Workouts have a different tone when they start early in the morning in the dark. Working out in the dark makes me feel like I am taking on the darkness in the world, but more importantly, the darkness inside of me. I moved from only visualizing my family during my workout to visualizing the demons and darkness seeking to attack my family and me. They represented different things: porn, temptation, sickness, doubt, worry, guilt, and shame. All of these things seek to destroy and distract a man from God's Will for him.

There is so much darkness we all face. There are things from our childhood and our adult past. There is guilt and shame from where you are right now. The minute you start fighting your way out of the PIT, know that the serpents will come for you. The minute you turn down a drink at the company party, someone will question you. When you retire early, rather than staying out with co-workers of the opposite sex, you will be noticed. When you start to try to relax in the hotel room, you will see porn on the pay-per-view. You're probably even feeling resistance right now, just reading this book and trying any of the missions. The war against the self never ends. The demons that want to keep you right where you are will be on the prowl the minute you start moving towards integrity and light. The difference is that now you have a weapon, and you can use it daily.

The Spiritual Warfare Protocol is an offensive weapon to align your heart, soul, and body in defense of your kingdom.

The good news is that you have nothing to fear. It's time to cause some casualties.

This next practice will show you how.

MISSION ACTION PLAN:

SPIRITUAL WARFARE PROTOCOL (SWP)

I'd ask you to just trust the process on this. Follow the steps and see what you find. I have found in over 600 sessions that this formula works to generate massive power.

1. Start time is in the dark, 60 minutes before sunrise.

2. Find a place outside.

3. You will perform a bodyweight workout that will take you at least 20 minutes. Ideally, it will include burpees. There is a sample workout called "The Eric" listed below.

4. Bring your headphones and use an app that will allow you to listen to The Bible in audio format.

5. Turn on your audio Scripture and start your workout.

6. As you execute the workout, every five or ten reps will be "for" someone. In other words, every time you do reps, you are intentionally "giving" them to someone. I use the visual image of "circling" my wife and daughters with reps. I have two daughters so I will often circle each daughter with five reps and then circle my wife with five reps for a total of 15.

7. As you perform these reps and go through the workout, be open to the revelations that will come and as you "hear" things in your mind and heart. Open your phone app or journal ,write them down quickly, and then get back into the workout.

8. GO TO WAR in the workout and push yourself under the frame of the reps being "for your family." BE AGGRESSIVE!

9. Write down the time it took to complete the workout, your experience, and what you felt after the session in a journal or the notes on your phone.

SAMPLE BODYWEIGHT WORKOUT "THE ERIC"

This workout was created in honor of Dr. Eric Cerwin, who passed away suddenly on November 17, 2019. He was on that hill with me as part of Warrior Week 38. He was as soft-spoken as he was full of love. I saw him find the courage to find the truth. "The Eric" uses a principle of 600 reps based on a practice given to me by strength coach Terence Mitchell from South Africa, who passed away on October 27, 2021. I'm including this to honor both of them.

50 x Flat out burpees

50 x Pushups

50 x Jump Squats

50 x Hindu Pushups

50 x Situps

50 x Mountain Climbers

2 Rounds (600 reps)

Modification:

If you are not ready for the entire 600 reps, cut the workout in half and do one round. Or, do 25 reps per exercise for two rounds.

Record your time for the workout. Now you've set a baseline. The game is now to work on beating that baseline each time you do the workout, even if it's just by a second or two. You are your own competition.

For more resources and workouts go to:

www.thesaleswar.com/weapons

_____

CONCLUSION

Your body is a gift.

Stop sacrificing it at the altar of your business targets or your quota. Stop using it to sedate and hide from the Truth about your situation.

Instead, see it as a weapon that you can use NOW. Regardless of what shape you find yourself in at this very moment, you can start to use this weapon today by following the principles that have been outlined here. These practices will align your body, heart, and spirit in a way that will deliver power into every area of your life, not the least of which is your business.

Do the work, and you will feel the difference.

Your energy is everything. When your body, heart, and spirit are aligned, you are prepared. You are prepared for the calls. You are prepared for the big presentation. You are prepared to connect and be present with your wife and children. You are prepared for anything. You are battle-ready.

Follow these practices and use the weapon of your body. Let it be a focal point of this alignment and a pathway to a higher energetic state. You can access it every day. This energy of alignment is the rarest of commodities in people. Your prospects, clients, and your family *will feel it.* Your prospects *will buy* your certainty and integrity in yourself.

Your certainty is most powerfully expressed in your ability as a business person, spouse, or parent to **hold space** for others. When you have practiced using the Weapons of The Spirit, The Heart, and The Body to access this power, you have positioned yourself to deploy the final weapon: **The Weapon of Presence.**

CHAPTER 7

THE WEAPON OF PRESENCE

"The Lord will fight for you,

and you have only to be silent."

Exodus 14:14

THE WEAPON OF PRESENCE

The previous three **Weapons of The Spirit**, **Heart**, and **Body** are the foundational building blocks that allow you to draw the final sword: the *Weapon of Presence*. In fact, each of the three previous weapons was discovered in a moment of being present. The Weapon of the Spirit came from the shift of wanting to flee the lies in a corporate sales meeting to a meeting with the CEO of The Universe, where there are only two things to talk about: *thank you* and *will you*. The discovery of the Weapon of the Heart came from a moment of presence on a hill and in a children's graveyard. The Weapon of the Body was discovered by combining the first two weapons and, after thousands of reps, realizing that the body can be used as an access point to power and presence with ourselves.

What if the best way to prepare for your next big presentation wasn't staying up until 4:00 AM the night before? What if the best way to prepare was to pray, connect with your family, and set your body on fire with an intense workout? What if you never worried about what PowerPoints you were going to bring to the meeting? What if your only focus was building the power necessary to bring *presence*?

In the following sections, we're going to talk about what that looks like practically. You will be given examples of what is possible when you deploy this weapon in sales and life. Then you will be sent on a simple mission that will show you how you can experience the Weapon of Presence. Finally, you will be given a protocol to deploy this weapon and make it an ongoing practice in your life.

Initially, your sword of presence may be a bit dull. It takes reps, but there is a reward on the other side. There's no finish line on any of these weapons. Your reward for continuing the work will be the absolute certainty of your ability to deploy into any marketplace, any condition, and deliver results. It won't happen the way the world teaches that it should. The world demands a constant grind. The systems of the world are calling for you to sacrifice your body, your family, and your spirit at the feet of the idol of the number. Instead, your reward will come when you learn how to live in that world *beyond quota*, beyond the targets others have set for you. When you create a world that is in alignment with God, with family, and with your soul *first*, massive results in business and life *just happen*.

In the next section, you find examples of how The Weapon of Presence leads to multi-million business deals in the middle of COVID, and how this weapon can also save a life. I honor you for continuing this far in the book. Don't quit. The Weapon of Presence will deliver business production, but it can also lead to finding *purpose, not by might nor by power, but by His Spirit.*

GO BENEATH THE SURFACE

2006: GKN AEROSPACE, North America HQ
St. Louis, MO

"We *really* hate you guys," said Dave, the bearded and grizzled NC programming manager. He leaned forward in his chair behind his paper-covered desk and glared at me and my partner Larry.

I looked down at my shoes to avoid his hard stare. I noticed that a sharp titanium chip had lodged itself in the bottom of my shoe. I stepped on it during our shame-filled walk through the massive manufacturing floor where 5-axis milling machines cut through metal at high speed 24/7. The machines were the size of city buses. The air in Dave's office smelled of NC machine lubricant.

"You *IDIOTS* nearly killed our entire F-15 production schedule last year!" Dave was built like a fullback, and he was getting angrier with every minute he spent looking at us. He walked out and slammed the door. Larry, who was my solutions engineer, looked at me with wide eyes as if to say, "What the hell have you gotten me into, bro?!" We didn't say a word.

It was uncomfortable, but I was willing to take the abuse. It had taken me eight months to get our company back into this account. I was a 29-year-old rookie at INCAT, a reseller of computer-aided design/manufacturing (CAD/CAM) software and consulting services. As one of my first assignments, my first sales mentor, Brian Cox, had given me the mission of getting back into into a major target and problem account. The account was one of the largest aerospace suppliers in North America and was strategic to the aerospace practice we were building at INCAT. It was a marquee account, but they hated us. The previous sales rep assigned to the account had made some mistakes with the software licensing, causing fifty of their NC machine programmers, who operated at a burden rate of $200 an hour, to be down for two weeks. My predecessor's mistake had cost the organization an untold amount of overhead, engineering expense, and labor costs. It also cost them their reputation with their own clients.

The door to Dave's office suddenly swung open, and in marched five large and very angry NC programmers. The air in the room got heavier. Dave turned around and left without saying a word. They verbally beat the hell out of me and my colleague, Larry Khuen, for the catastrophic license outage.

I had worked every possible angle to get into the account. The first meetings I got were with lower-level IT consultants who weren't even employees. I would fly the three hours from LAX to St. Louis multiple times just to suffer the humiliation of only being invited into the tiny meeting room in the front lobby. I didn't even get to go into the main facility. Like I said, they hated us.

I knew this meeting with Dave was my one chance. The trauma of that mistake was burned in the collective memory of the NC programming team. It felt like a firing squad. Larry and I had to just sit there and *be present* and take it. Any defensiveness on our part would have surely gotten us both thrown from the second story. When the beating was over, the men walked out, and Dave walked back in.

He sat down behind his desk. His eyes had softened.

"We need to buy five licenses of CATIA NC software."

Wait. What?

There was a moment of disbelief as his statement hung in the air. I couldn't believe there might be a chance to capture ANY sale after this. The five licenses that they wanted would have been worth over $200,000, and I would have easily hit my quota and bonuses for the quarter. All those months of humiliation were about to pay off! I felt a massive push to jump on the bait. But somehow, in that moment, I had the presence of mind to just hold and wait. And instead of saying, "How soon can we get the order?" I said, "Ok, five licenses of CATIA NC software. Got it. What else would be ideal for you?"

Dave looked at me, took a deep breath, and paused for another long moment.

His face continued to relax. He wasn't terrifying anymore. Had his dark brown beard been white, he would have looked like Santa Clause with a cheerful twinkle in his eye.

He looked back at me and said, "Well, next month, we're preparing for a major bid on the new project for the Navy. We should probably build out a strategy around that."

"Would you like help with that?" I responded.

He said, "Yes, let's set up a meeting to talk about that." I said, "Good deal. I'll bring Sam." Sam Abu Hamdan was my other right-hand man, a Ph.D., and technical genius.

"Sounds good!" he said. "Be sure to send me the quote for the software. We need to buy that ASAP. Would you guys like to go to lunch? There's good BBQ at Bandana's and Indian food a mile away. Let's do Indian. I'm hungry! Let's go!"

Dave's team ended up winning the Navy project eight months later. The plan for software and services we helped them construct enhanced their bid. The client won the multi-year contract and we won several million in services. It created one of the largest contracts that our organization had closed with any aerospace company at that time. We blew out all of my numbers and got awarded the "Kill the Competition" award at our sales conference.

I realized later that if I had acted out of desperation to grab the five software licenses and not ask another question, I would have missed the multi-million dollar contract in services and technology that came in the next year.

Salespeople jump on the first problem they think they can solve for a prospect. It's a jump of desperation that closes down the space for the prospect to think and discover. Dave discovered that he needed much more than the five software licenses, but he would not have had that revelation at that moment had I opened my mouth. When salespeople talk instead of listening, they rob themselves, and more importantly, their client, of discoveries, insights, and potential game-changing modes of production that would have been available had they just held the space and kept their mouth closed and their ears open.

I held the space accidentally with Dave. Perhaps I was shell-shocked from the verbal beating we'd just received, or I was just so surprised there was an opportunity for a sale that I didn't have the words. I didn't create that space with presence intentionally. It was clearly all God's provision. The sale was great, but the lesson was far more valuable.

Instead of $200,000, we found *millions* in the *space* just *below* the surface.

What might be just below the surface of your next sales meeting? What might be just below the surface of your next conversation with your spouse?

True mastery of The Weapon of Presence comes not through an accidental manifestation but instead through an intentional deployment. Another level of awareness and capacity is required, but when deployed, you can become something truly unique to your prospects and clients.

BECOMING THE AGENT OF REVELATION

2019 - Central US, Academic Medical Center

I could feel the migraine forming like a 12-inch nail driving through my right eye. The boardroom on the top floor of the hospital tower was beautiful, but the lights were a bright white temperature. I had forgotten my special blue light-blocking glasses and was paying for it.

It had been thirteen years since the events at the aerospace manufacturer in St. Louis. I was now selling technology and services into the healthcare industry. I found myself in the executive boardroom of one of the leading academic health systems in the country with Jennifer, the new SVP of marketing.

Jennifer and her team sat across from me and my colleague, Christine, at the large, sleek boardroom table. Jennifer was faced with the big challenge of unifying a politically divided organization into a new digital strategy. Jennifer brought a level of intellect, vision, and passion that made her an outlier vs. most healthcare executives. I had seen only a few executives like her in the five years I'd been selling to healthcare systems. Executives like her are extremely rare, and I have learned to appreciate them. Most healthcare executives didn't want to rock the boat; they wanted to keep their feet firmly planted and maintain the status quo. Jennifer and her team were willing to blow up the boat for the sake of the patient.

The objective of our meeting that day was to simply create the space for them to clarify where they wanted to go. Christine and I came in with no presentation, just a framework of powerful questions. We didn't present anything. We didn't talk. We didn't solve any problems for them. Instead, we asked powerful questions. I listened to what they had to say, and I mirrored it back verbatim. We were *present* and held space with all the focus on them.

After four hours of holding the space, the white lights had kick-started the migraine, but I was committed to continuing the process and staying *present*. I also refused to even hint that I was in any pain. The objective was to protect the space for Jennifer and her team. I had done this enough times to know that if we just held firm, a discovery would come.

"Wait a minute!" Jennifer slammed her hand down on the table in a sudden moment of revelation.

"This means we don't have to build that other website," she said excitedly.

"Yes, that appears to be the case," I responded.

"Ok. Wow. This entire time I thought we had to do that too," she said. "This will save us a million dollars and a year to get there! This is huge!"

The revelation was complete.

Four months later, we signed a multi-year services contract. Providentially, the project arrived just in time to support the organization as COVID19 arrived twelve months later. All the momentum was based on Jennifer's revelations. Her revelation had strategic implications for the entire organization, and impacted tens of thousands of patients. That moment in our meeting would have never happened if we had filled the space with our words or solutions. The solution she found was *hers*; we were just the guides. We were just the **Agents of Revelation.**

The Weapon of Presence allows you to be not only a guide to your prospect or client but an agent of their revelation. In other words, when they discover an insight or perspective that they had not seen before due to the space *you* created for them in a conversation, your product is only part of what they are buying. They are buying the most rare and unique product that no other competitor can offer: the *revelation* that *they found* because of *your presence.*

FIND WHAT'S HIDDEN IN THE SILENCE

April 29, 2020 - COVID 19 GLOBAL PANDEMIC - Dallas, TX,
Conference call with a national health system: 3:15 PM

The world was in meltdown. The COVID-19 virus was spreading worldwide, the President had declared a national emergency, and the stock market had crashed just a few weeks before. The media was a daily torrent of fear, highlighting all of the social and political unrest that comes with every election year. Every industry was retreating, and businesses were all focused on survival. The healthcare industry and hospitals, in particular, were being crushed. Many hospitals closed their doors to anyone other than the most seriously ill and COVID patients. Healthcare organizations had moved into all-hands-on-deck mode and were managing the crisis day-by-day. It was hardly an ideal time to be selling marketing services to hospitals.

"Julie, what questions do you have?" I asked.

Two of my colleagues and I had just finished presenting a strategy and timeline for the deployment of marketing and digital advertising services to one of the largest healthcare systems in the country. It was a huge account for us and a complex, high-stakes solution for the client. It was a miracle that we were even talking. Most hospitals had frozen all spending, and the last thing they would spend money on was marketing.

Julie was the executive leading the deal. I love working with people like her. She was sharp, dynamic, honest, and powerful. She was another exception in the world of healthcare marketing. She was full of integrity and, as a result, fearless. She was also deafeningly quiet on the other side of the conference line.

I knew that this was the critical point. The energy of the deal was right. All we had to do was just keep our mouths shut.

Hold. Hold. Hold.

"Julie, you're being awfully quiet!" my colleague suddenly interjected into the silence.

The interjection instantly started to collapse the thinking space inside the conversation. The silence was too uncomfortable, and anxiety crept in.

I furiously typed out a text message to my teammate.

"Please. Quiet."

I brought all my force of will to the moment. I closed my eyes and pictured the three people on the phone. I couldn't see them, but I could feel them. I wanted my colleagues' anxiety to subside, and I wanted Julie to have *uninterrupted* space to think.

"Well, we have this other agreement we have to make, so I guess that's something we need to consider," she said off-handedly. That next revelation ended up being worth millions of dollars.

My colleagues didn't recognize the importance of this statement at the moment, but I did. In the quiet, still presence, I immediately knew Julie's revelation had just given both companies a huge leverage point that would create a better and more powerful scenario for all of us.

This simple moment would have been lost in any other conversation. This *revelation* that was *just below the surface* enabled us to expand deal value by 300% and close it, in the middle of a global pandemic, with a $13.9 million commitment. It was a massive win for the client and our company.

The next day, I moved the deal from the "I know You can, will You?" column in my journal to the "Thank You" column. I had been meeting with the CEO of the Universe on this one for a while. When a deal like this closes in the middle of a global pandemic and economic meltdown, there's only one executive who is *really* getting it done. I made sure to thank Him.

Know this: the big deals, the really big deals, the impossible deals, are hidden in moments of silence. Inside those moments, there is no competition. You create your own personal blue ocean.

When you wield the Weapon of Presence, you become the creator of moments of silence and the agent of revelation for your prospects and clients. The three deals mentioned here were worth over twenty million in commitments. Twenty million in sales came down to three single moments in time and space that would never have happened if the space had been collapsed by my own uncertainty, anxiety, or self-focus.

I encourage you to be the man who intentionally creates that presence and masters it. You will be absolutely unstoppable. You'll dominate in any marketplace. Your sales will increase, but you will value them less. The idols of achievement and sales awards will fall away. You will begin to realize that your true worth is not in your sales numbers but instead in your willingness to surrender to be an instrument of God.

MAKE THE CALL, NOW.

I was with my family on a Sunday afternoon preparing for church when a red social media alert appeared on my phone that said, "Chris was live."

I had met Chris at a Wake Up Warrior event twelve months previously. We had argued passionately over the existence of God and UFOs. He was adamant that God didn't exist but that UFOs were real. (It turns out he was right about one of those.) Susanna and I were trying to get the girls ready, so I didn't really have time to check social media alerts, but I felt prompted to check this one. There was a gut-level feeling of urgency about it.

I clicked on the video and saw Chris's very swollen face. In the video, he was drunk and rambling. His marriage was imploding, and his wife had just kicked him out. His children were away, so he was alone.

The urgency in my gut grew. I felt a hard push in my spirit.

Call Chris. Now.

I called him and left him a voicemail. I had a million other things going on at that moment, but I was clearly told to call him. I called again. No answer. I felt a pull to let it go and just focus on getting the kids to church on time, but then there was a tiny moment of presence, and I felt it again:

Call him.

I sent him a video call this time. He picked up.

"Hey bro, I'm not doing well." His eyes were red, and his cheeks were puffy. His words were slurred, "They are all gone."

I simply told him I was praying for him and that I was there for him. I tried my best to encourage him not to drink anything else and hold fast. I felt like I was carrying a message for him. The prompt came back, this time with the message.

"You are NOT ALONE," I told him.

I encouraged him to get some rest and told him to call me if he needed anything. We hung up after a few minutes, and I went back to rushing the girls to our afternoon church service. I didn't think of it again after that.

Over a year later, I found myself at a large conference Warrior event, and there was a call for any man who had been fighting the war of sobriety to come to the stage. There were about 3000 men in the room, and everyone who didn't take the stage would honor these men for taking a stand against their addictions. A huge roar of applause went up as approximately fifty men went up to the stage.

In the middle of the group, seventy-five feet away, I found the eyes of Chris. I had not seen or talked to him since that video call. He looked completely different. His energy was bright. He had lost at least 40 pounds. He stood tall. We locked eyes, and his eyes were ablaze. He didn't just look different: he was a different man. As the crowd rose and applauded, with eyes locked, I put my hand to my heart. Chris put his hand to his heart, and it was a moment of intense and complete presence.

A few minutes later, Chris walked off the stage straight to where I was standing in the huge crowd. Without a word, he gave me a huge bear hug. Then he leaned back and locked eyes with me and put his hand on my heart.

"Brother, you saved my life."

I knew exactly what he meant. What is understood doesn't need to be explained.

"No, brother, it wasn't me," I said with tears in my eyes. "I just listened and acted when God prompted me."

In the years that followed that moment, I've been able to witness Chris become a master at listening and acting. He has transformed his life in incredible ways, both as a father and businessman. We are brothers to this day, and he is a constant reminder of how God is always speaking to me. I must seek to be still and ACT when I feel led.

The Weapon of Presence is more than a powerful business weapon. The Weapon of Presence is ultimately where we enter into a place where we can hear and listen and decide to act on what God is calling us to do at that moment. What God calls us to do, that we so often tune out, is so much bigger than what we have for ourselves.

Ultimately, the Weapon of Presence is about creating a space and surrender where you are an instrument of God.

But what does that actually look like in a sales conversation?

In the next section, we will talk about the principles of the Weapon of Presence. You will be given examples so that you can learn how this Weapon applies, not only to business conversations but to all domains of life. Think of it as presence-based selling and presence-based living. This is a lifestyle that is centered around intentionally opening and creating spaces so that God can speak into you and you get the gift of ACTING.

CHAPTER 7

WIELDING
THE WEAPON
OF PRESENCE

"Ask, and it will be given to you;

seek, and you will find;

knock, and it will be opened to you."

Matthew 7:7

WIELDING THE WEAPON OF PRESENCE

Business in its purest form is an act of creation. Sales is an act of creation. Our ultimate role as salespeople is to be a guide that helps others create.

The weapon of presence is an instrument of creation. We create what God calls us to create and help others do the same. We've all been built with this innate capacity, but we've mostly forgotten it. We must go through a process of awakening and remembering this part of our nature. We must remember how to create as a child does. When a child creates, they demonstrate the act of creating in its purest form...that is, to LISTEN and ACT. I see this with my daughter Annie Grace. She gets an idea and then just builds it. She has a feeling and just draws it.

In a child, there is almost no friction between inspiration and manifestation. It's closer to the way God creates.

God *speaks* reality into existence. There is no friction between His thought and creation.

God speaks, and it is.

And calling to him a child, he put him in the midst of them and said, "Truly, I say to you, unless you turn and become like children, you will never enter the kingdom of heaven. - Matthew 18, 2-4

This is quite the opposite of what we do as adults. We live in a headspace of confusion and self. Living in this place blocks us from receiving the Divine Signal that God is broadcasting ALL THE TIME. So, we fall into the ego-driven feedback loop of "I've got to do this all myself and grind through it." Sound familiar?

This loop inevitably leads to the pit of guilt and shame when we fail. We operate on an ego-driven feedback loop instead of a signal from Him. This happened repeatedly as I tried to do this book all myself. This was my own personal war in writing this book. In fact, this chapter was perhaps the most difficult battle. Old patterns reemerged as I continued to over-think and over-prepare in my uncertainty. All the voices were there in the dark nights and dark mornings saying:

"Who are you to write a book?"

"No one cares what you're going to say."

"It has to be perfect, or it will hurt your reputation."

The only way through it was to LET GO, quit trying to do it all myself, and ASK HIM to carry me through it. I had to draw The Weapon Of Presence myself, and in doing so, I discovered a deeper level of the nature of its principles.

What was really happening in those moments, in those big business deals, or even writing this book? Creation. So how do we move from a place from accidental to intentional creation (and sales domination)?

The Bible gives us the formula in the Gospel of Matthew:

"Ask, and it will be given to you; seek, and you will find; knock, and it will be opened to you. For everyone who asks receives, and the one who seeks finds, and to the one who knocks it will be opened." - Matthew 7:7

It's a simple formula that Jesus Christ lays out as recorded in the Gospel of Matthew:

ASK

SEEK

KNOCK

Later, scripture adds one more: ACT.

But be doers of the word, and not hearers only, deceiving your-selves. - James 1:22

I transition this into the following sequential formula:

TO ASK	=	INTENTION
TO SEEK	=	CONNECTION
TO KNOCK	=	REVELATION
TO ACT	=	ACTION

In the following section, we're going to break down each of these principles and look at how they play out. Doing so will also reveal why **The Weapons of The Spirit, The Heart,** and **The Body** are so effective. If you've completed the missions and are living out the protocols, even in the smallest way, *you have been drawing **The Weapon of Presence** all along.*

THE FOUR PRINCIPLES

The Principle of INTENTION - In the chaos of our minds, egos, and the distraction of the world, accidental creation rarely happens. We have TO CHOOSE to create. This is the first step. This is where the war begins. Choosing to create is a declaration of our desire to select HIS signal over everything else. When we draw the weapon, it means we are taking a stand and seeking the resistance. The work of ASKING is to acknowledge that we do not have the answer, and that is where the process begins. *Asking creates space.* When we ask, we are given. God guarantees it.

The Principle of CONNECTION - Once we have acted on the intention and are ASKING, we have automatically moved into a place of humility. "To ask" is to acknowledge that we don't have the answer and that the answer must come from something outside of ourselves. Asking moves our egos, our minds, and our stories out of the way and clears a space for the divine connection that happens in our hearts. Your heart is always connected to God. Your heart is other-focused. Thus to connect with God, simply seek Him. When you seek, you will find. God guarantees it.

The Principle of REVELATION - God promises that when we knock, the door will be opened. When we ask the question, and the answer arrives in our hearts, it is then that we are given divine information. What a gift it is to have the unseen Truth revealed. Revelation is the ultimate product. When we knock, the door will always be opened. God guarantees it.

The Principle of ACTION - Once we receive the revelation, we are then faced with a choice. We can choose to CREATE and act upon the revelation or do nothing. This is our AGENCY as beings with free will. We must manifest the revelation into our reality. We must invite and welcome the Spirit. We must viciously seek to align ourselves with God's will. When we ACT, we must make the ethereal, temporal. We are agents of His kingdom on earth.

We know that most men hear, but they do not listen, let alone act. And that is why the man who listens and acts will be set apart. He is the man who does not deceive himself. He is the man who wields the Truth.

Let's look at each of these principles in the context of the three Weapons and respective missions and protocols from the previous chapters. If you haven't completed the missions, go back, complete them, and return.

The Weapon of The Spirit:
"Meeting with The CEO of The Universe"

THE INTENTION (SEEK) - The intention is set in the act of scheduling the meeting on your calendar. You are taking a stand. You are stating, "This time is for me and Him to connect."

THE CONNECTION (ASK) - The agenda of "Thank you" and "Will You" (along with the two cups of coffee) move you into a connection with your heart. Gratitude is the fastest shortcut to connection in the heart.

THE REVELATION (KNOCK) - There are revelations in the meeting of all the things you have to thank Him for (i.e., "wow, I have so much to be thankful for") and what you are prompted to ask for. There are also revelations that start stacking each week as you look back on the things you *asked for* in previous meetings that you have now been *given.* Each of these is evidence of God's presence with YOU and His faithfulness to YOU.

THE ACTION (CREATION) - The act of writing the things you are asking for is an act of creation. The literal pen to paper is manifestation. The commitment to set the next meeting with Him on the calendar is an act of creation. The commitment to do those things you hear during the meeting are all acts of creation.

The Weapon of The Heart:
"Daily Notes of Love, Honor, and Appreciation"

THE INTENTION (SEEK) - In this daily practice, we set the intention to search our hearts and consider why we love, honor, and appreciate members of our family.

THE CONNECTION (ASK) - At that moment, when our heart responds, we are connected.

THE REVELATION (KNOCK) - Then we "get" the answer in a revelation... i.e., "I love you because....xyz."

THE ACTION (CREATION) - When we put that revelation into physical words and share it, it manifests into our reality in a message... this is AN ACT of Divine CREATION.

The Weapon of The Body: "Spiritual Warfare Protocol"

THE INTENTION (SEEK) - We are not working out to get in shape but instead to get in power through connection with Him. We seek to go to war with the darkness and demons that seek to destroy us. We set an intention to go to war against our flesh.

THE CONNECTION (ASK) - We connect to God and our loved ones by listening to scripture during the workout and orienting our hearts by saying, "these reps are for..."

THE REVELATION (KNOCK) - In the protocol, we experience messages and revelations. We are given clarity. When we ask, "who are these reps for?" it is revealed.

THE ACTION (CREATION) - Each rep, each pushup, each burpee is a physical act of creation. Each rep is focused spiritual intention. The protocol itself is an act of creation that is manifested in a physical prayer.

All of these missions and protocols align you to create more space, power, and ALIGNMENT with God. But to what end?

Consider this: The ultimate reason to grow your own power and capacity to create is so that you can use it to *serve others* in creating and growing their power and capacity to create. Your results in business are directly proportional to the results you help others create.

Creation is the core of our true nature as children of God. It is what we are called to do as husbands, fathers, leaders, men, and as salespeople. In the same way that God helps us create when we find presence with Him, we assist others in their acts of creation when we create presence with them.

> *"Nor do people light a lamp and put it under a basket, but on a stand, and it gives light to all in the house. In the same way, let your light shine before others, so that they may see your good works and give glory to your Father who is in heaven." - Matthew 5: 15-17*

USING THE WEAPONS and CREATING THE FIELD

The Weapon of Presence creates a field in space. Fields can be small or large. They can be weak or strong. They can be a trap when they collapse, or they can be a refuge when they hold. We often hear about the idea of what it means to "hold space," but what does that really mean? I would define it as follows: To *"create space"* is to intentionally create a set of conditions where there is an awareness and non-reactivity to internal or external stimuli. To *"hold space"* is to have the capacity to hold that state of non-reactivity regardless of stimuli.

Every one of the Weapons creates a field of altered space that is different from normal space, and there is a distinct *inside* and *outside*.

This is to "create the field."

We live every moment in a state of self-selected reactivity most of our lives. Thus the first step in using this weapon is to build our own capacity to create and hold space with ourselves. Until we can create and hold space with ourselves, we'll never have the capacity to hold it very long for another human.

But why is that even important, and how in the hell is it relevant to the conversation of sales? I'm glad you asked.

BECOME THE MOST PRESENT MAN IN THE ROOM

My old mantra before a big presentation used to be, "I'll outwork everyone and be the most prepared man in the room!" This is what led to the all-nighters and hundreds of slides so I could be ready for anything.

Now I commit to simply being ***the most present man in the room.***

The present man can see the small details, he picks up on innuendo, sees the Truth, and spots the lies. He feels the energy of others.

The present man wins the big deals because he is the catalyst for their creation. The end.

We've all been near people who had "a presence" when they entered the room. Guess what? You were inside their field. You were reacting to them, and they were *just there* with you. I'm sure you can think of a time when you've felt this. Pets and very small children are some of the best at this. They are willing to *just be* present with you. You might have experienced this with a great orator or even a colleague. It might have been the reason you fell in love with your partner.

The alignment of spirit, heart, and body creates the conditions of a powerful presence. Thus, my preparation for a big meeting is not staying up all night but hitting my workout, orienting my heart to my family, and aligning with my God before stepping into the room.

My commitment is to always enter a conversation with the highest vibrational energy possible because it allows me to be of the *most service* to whoever I encounter. This could be a prospect, a client, my wife, or my children. I challenge you to make this your commitment.

In that place of power, when you show up, your presence is *felt* by others. From that foundational power, you are able to *move the field* to enclose others and invite them into a space away from the noise and chaos of their lives and into a space of revelation and creation.

Presence is one of the highest gifts one person can give to another: to have the capacity to create a field of space that another can step into and then protect the space so that they can find clarity, revelation, and the guidance to take action and create.

This is one of the highest functions of a salesperson. When we are at our most aligned, this is what we do. It's presence-based selling.

In all of the previously mentioned stories, the prospects found their revelations because I had simply facilitated an energetic space that was quiet enough to allow them to discover them.

"I guess we need to build a plan for the big program."

"This is going to save me a million dollars!"

"This would help with our commitment."

All of these moments of revelation for my clients ultimately led to the creation of massive value for their companies, themselves, my company, and ultimately me and my family. In every one of those deals, there was no competition. There was never any doubt that the deals would come through. The deals created record revenue numbers. They smashed quotas and targets. But that was never the point. When a man plays the game at this level, he is not driven by the targets his sales manager gives him. He lives beyond quota. He puts his company in HIS field. He lives for the bigger cosmic game that is at work. He lives for the moments that contribute to his heavenly reward.

Moments like the one with Chris and his call for help.

In the following section, you will have three missions to apply these principles. You've made it this far. Now it's time to bring it all together and integrate the weapons first, for yourself, then for others, and then with The CEO of The Universe.

During each mission, we'll practice each of the principles. The objective is to create an awareness where you can see these principles at work in every sales conversation, every moment with your children or wife, and with yourself and God.

Each mission will use the Intention, Connection, Revelation, Creation framework.

It's time to be doers, not just hearers. Let's go.

MISSIONS

MISSION 1: BE STILL - PRESENCE WITH YOURSELF - CREATE A FIELD WITH YOU

This first mission may be the shortest, but it also may be the most difficult. You're just going to take a few moments to be present with YOU. How often are we really present with ourselves? Most of our lives, we avoid this because we don't want to look at the truth of where we are. When people ask us, "How are you doing?" our standard answer is, "I'm doing good. How are you?" But, let's face it, most of the time, that's a lie. Our willingness to examine ourselves and stand in the truth of who and where we are right now is the foundation for everything else. We've got to have the courage to look at our reality with no judgment and just see "what is." This is to move to a place where we are no longer willing to remain blind to the truth but instead seek a place where "I am aware that I am aware."

To do this, you are simply going to be still.

MISSION ACTION PLAN

STEP 1: Wherever you are, take out your journal, a piece of scrap paper, or your phone and write the words, "My intention for the next fifteen minutes is to be still."

STEP 2: Set a timer for 15 minutes. Start the timer and close your eyes.

STEP 3: When the timer goes off, open your eyes.

STEP 4: Write down one thing you learned or observed from the experience.

RETURN & REPORT

What did you experience during this mission? It's amazing how seeking to "be still" reveals how "unstill" we actually are. You may have had thoughts or worries come rushing in. You may have been aware of a noise in your environment or a feeling in your body. You may have felt emotion for a loved one. I feel all of these when I practice this mission. The point is not to judge each thought, feeling, or observation, but rather just be aware of them and hold the space of your field for yourself by being non-reactive. Hold lightly to each thought, emotion, or feeling as it enters your awareness and then, let it go. If you are reading this and thinking, "Well, I did that terribly" or "I did that well," let that go too. It doesn't matter.

The most important thing was to complete Step #4. (Did you do it? If not, go back and do it and then write down what you learned from the experience.)

By choosing to put pen to paper, you just took the ethereal and made it temporal. This was an act of creation.

In this mission, you've just practiced the four principles.

STEP 1: You set your INTENTION: "to be still."

STEP 2: You found CONNECTION with yourself (even if you connected with an "unstill self").

STEP 3: You were given a REVELATION in what you observed.

STEP 4: You committed an act of CREATION by writing down what you observed.

You created a space. You held it (weakly or strongly). You found a revelation in that space. You turned that revelation into creation by writing it down.

You did this inside a field of presence with yourself. It's important to recognize that had you not used your intention to create this field of time and space, you would not have received this revelation you were just given or the creation (the notes on the page) you just created.

Creating this field of presence becomes easier relative to the amount of power and alignment you've created in yourself beforehand. The alignment of spirit, heart, and body makes the creation of moments of stillness exponentially easier and more powerful. It is from this place that you can have "presence to spare" to serve another person. We'll explore this in the next mission. We'll look at this specifically in the context of a sales or business conversation, but also how it actually applies to any interaction with another human.

MISSION 2: THE MOST PRESENT MAN IN THE ROOM

In this mission, we will take the power of all the weapons and combine them to create power. This power will allow you to bring your maximum potential presence into a conversation with another person. We will combine our heightened personal resonance with four powerful questions and a conversational process. This will serve as a framework of catalysts for revelation for the person you serve. As a salesperson, think of this person as a prospect or client. If you're not in sales, this other person could just as easily be a business partner, your wife, or even your child.

This framework led directly to my clients' revelations converting into millions in sales and value for their companies.

This mission will require that you have a specific person in mind, someone to whom you want to bring this gift of revelation. Who do you have in mind? Check your calendar.

STEP 1: GET IN POWER.

On the day of your meeting, presentation, or conversation, draw all the weapons. Wake up before sunrise and align your body, heart, and soul. Use the Spiritual Warfare Protocol. Write notes to your family. Spend at least a few minutes with the CEO of The Universe. Thank Him and ask Him.

STEP 2: SET THE INTENTION

Moments before the meeting set your intention on how you will serve the other person (or people). Specifically, I suggest that you set an intention "to guide and shepherd." Write it down. This is vital because it helps you orient from the typical self-focused mindset of the sales-person, which is often "to persuade" or "to sell." Then, you can orient your heart to the outcomes for the other person.

The following question brings this state into reality:

> "Relative to our time together today, what would be your ideal outcomes?"

This is a powerful way to begin any conversation. It signals to the other person that you are there FOR THEM and that a unique space is being formed (i.e., "our time together today").

STEP 3: CONNECTION - CREATE AND HOLD THE FIELD

It's vital to note that the process is as important as the questions them-selves. Before we get to the questions, let's look at the process and cadence.

The process and cadence of your questions and responses are what create and hold the field BOTH of you. In these conversations, you'll be tempted to talk instead of listening. You'll be tempted to consider opportunities for yourself above those of the client. In those moments, return to the process and use it as your home base. The process is also key to the CONNECTION aspect of the formula.

The questioning process involves three components:

1. Question/Response

2. Listening & Recording

3. Replay

This creates a circular energetic exchange between you and the other person.

This is what it looks like in a conversation:

You :	Question
Person:	Response
You :	Replay the Person's Response
Person:	Confirmation of Your Replay
You:	Question
Person:	Response
You :	Replay the Person's Response
Person:	Confirmation of Your Replay

The CONNECTION between the two people in the conversation deepens as you work to continually cycle through this pattern and maintain the energetic circle. When you do this effectively with any other human, you build an energetic connection that sets the foundation for a relationship built on trust. When you demonstrate that you can hold the space, focus, and put their needs before yours, you lay a strong foundation.

DEEP QUESTIONING (The Iceberg)

How we ask questions is just as important as the questions themselves. It's important to know that the deepest, most powerful revelations are rarely visible from the surface.

Picture an iceberg: what we see on the surface is just a small piece of something much bigger, something deeper. What we initially see or hear from someone is never the whole story. There is always more under the surface that they may or may not be aware of. So when we question, we always ask the primary question, and after receiving a response, we continue with, "What else?" With each "What else?" the client gets to consider more and go deeper. New revelations will form. It's not unusual to hear their most powerful desires and deepest fears emerge after multiple circuits of the questions. The key is to know this ahead of time. Don't rob the client of the revelation that is just around the corner. Hold space. Listen and wait. The treasure is *beneath the surface.*

STEP 4: REVELATION
USE THE MILLION-DOLLAR QUESTIONS

The following questions were based on a single day's training that I had early in my sales career from one of my sales mentors, Rory Clark. This simple questioning process has created millions of dollars in sales. I knew that the questions and the process worked, but it wasn't until much later that I discovered *why* they worked. The questions are a formula for artificially creating presence for salespeople who are, in general terms, an energetic, needy mess. Even if a salesperson had no concept of what was behind the scenes, if they ran the play, they would get results. The process works because the questions create space. The process holds space (even if you're an energetic mess), and eventually leads to revelation and creation. The questions and the process complete the entire arc of Intention, Connection, Revelation, and Creation.

After we've established that this space (i.e., "the field") is meant to serve the prospect or client, we can then invite them into the space and then be the guide for their own revelations (i.e., "move the field").

Most people are not really clear about what they want, what the problem is, or what's in their way. It often takes an outside observer to help them see what they cannot. This is what great coaches do for their clients. They help people see their own blind spots. And, it's no accident that it's exactly what the greatest salespeople do as well. In business, millions of dollars are hiding in the blind spots. Your job is to guide the client towards what they can't see.

Now that you understand what's going on behind the scenes, we're going to move into the war for REVELATION by using the Million Dollar Questions.

QUESTION 1: What are your desired outcomes?

QUESTION 2: What obstacles are preventing your desired outcomes?

QUESTION 3: What happens if things stay as they are and nothing changes?

QUESTION 4: When ideally would you like to see your desired outcomes achieved?

Earth-shattering, right? You probably use some form of these questions already, otherwise, you wouldn't be where you are as a successful sales executive! The distinction here is less about the questions and more about *why* they work and the final product: CONNECTION & REVELATION.

We're going to look behind the curtain so you can see what's really going on energetically. Let's look at what each of The Million Dollar Questions is actually doing for the person receiving the question.

QUESTION 1: What are your desired outcomes?

Effect of Question: Orients the client towards exploring a desired FUTURE STATE.

This question serves to orient the other person's mind away from a current state focus to a "desired future state," whatever that may be. This is counter to many sales approaches in that we **don't seek** to immediately uncover where the client is now. You've heard and asked the questions before at the beginning of a sales call, i.e., "What are you doing today? What software do you use now? Who do you currently use? Etc. etc." Even though your motives may feel other-focused, these current situation questions carry an intrinsic self-focus bias. The prospect knows that you're looking for problems you think you can solve. This collapses the field, and the prospect closes down. It feels like an interrogation. Instead, you expand the field for the client by asking them what they want and where they want to go.

QUESTION 2: What obstacles are preventing your desired outcomes?

Effect of Question: Revelation of current situation factors that are preventing the desired future state.

This question creates awareness of the distinct elements blocking their desired outcomes and creating a gap. This also creates awareness of the pain they feel because of the dissonance between their future desired state and the current situation.

QUESTION 3: What happens if things stay as they are and nothing changes?

Effect of Question: Revelation of the painful, emotional, or financial cost of staying where they are and exposing any unintended consequences of delay of action.

Most of the time, people know exactly what they need to be doing, but for some reason, they aren't doing it. We all do this. At any given time, there is something that we should start doing or stop doing, and yet we delay. We don't take action.

In the Book of Romans 7:15, Paul even laments about this, *"For I do not understand my own actions. For I do not do what I want, but I do the very thing I hate."*

When we ask ourselves the question, "What if things stay as they are?" we are forced to reorient from what's in the way, back into a future state focus. The difference this time is that instead of a desired future state, we are exploring the possibility of a future state to see if there is unrealized pain and consequence.

QUESTION 4: When ideally would you like to see your desired outcomes achieved?

Effect of Question: This question delivers revelation of what their desires are relative to time, outcome, and what beliefs they may have about what is possible. Once the desired outcomes have the desired achievement date, we are able to move the ethereal into the temporal. When a client says, "I'd like to see the project online by December first," they start the process of moving from revelation to creation. In a sales context, this information is valuable in establishing a time frame based on the client's desired outcomes that can be used to drive the sales process forward.

THE FINAL PRODUCT: CONNECTION & REVELATION

When these questions are combined with mirroring and deep questioning, there are almost always two results: Connection and Revelation. Again, connection forms from the circular energetic flow that happens as one person holds the space for the other and puts total focus on them using questions and mirroring. When this is done effectively, it's not unusual for both parties to feel positive feelings towards each other. The person you invited into your field may not be able to articulate why they like you now, but for some reason, they just feel like they do!

The other product is Revelation. Whether or not the revelations created in this space lead to an immediate opportunity for your company is irrelevant. If they do, that's great, but if not, that's ok too. The gift to the other person was the space for revelation. As long as you held the space, kept them safe in the field, and helped them find a new perspective or revelation, they are leaving with a gift, and you have been of service. It's not always about finding the big deal at the moment. It can take many of these conversations to triangulate on the blindspot or the opportunity you can uniquely solve, but every conversation provides value regardless. The work creates an opportunity that you uniquely solve because you helped the client *FIND* it.

And now, there is one final step to bring the mission full circle. You're about to learn a "hack" that can help the most desperate sales rookies or even the seasoned exec on a bad day.

THE PRESENCE HACK:
USE HANDWRITTEN VERBATIM NOTES

Regardless of the intensity of your commitment to put yourself in power, there will be tough days where everything is out of alignment. Maybe you just fought with your wife, or you feel the virus of scarcity coming in because the numbers are down. Maybe you just had a late night up with your baby, missed your workout, overslept, and the meeting is in 30 minutes. How can you get present when the conditions are anything but ideal?

I'm reminded of a quote that's often quoted by Navy Seals but originates from the Greek poet Archilochos, "We don't rise to the level of our expectations, we fall to the level of our training."

So when the pressure is on, and our energy is weak, we can fall back on a simple hack that creates presence, other-focus, and connection all in one practice: write handwritten verbatim notes.

Writing handwritten notes during the process does three things:

1. It requires a huge amount of mental energy and zeros in
    your focus, leaving no room for the self-focused
    impulses that want to creep in and collapse the
    space. In other words, it doesn't leave any room for
    you to think about "what you're gonna sell them" while
    they are talking.

2. We can't talk while writing, which further protects the
    space.

3. Finally, it focuses all of our energy on the other person's words, and they energetically feel this, especially when we mirror back their exact words.

In an age where there are now platforms that record sales calls or auto-transcribe conversations, my prediction is that presence and focus will become increasingly rare as sales reps are no longer asked to record the notes because the A.I. will do it.

This just creates bigger opportunities for the man with The Weapon of Presence.

STEP 5: CLOSE THE LOOP OF CREATION AND GIVE THEM BACK THE NOTES

Remember the act of creation in Mission 1 of simply writing down the revelation? You've literally been taking their revelations and performing an act of creation by recording them. All of the written notes you've captured during the conversation have been in service to the client. Once they've been recorded, the best practice is to send those notes to the client within 24 hours. There's something magical about this process. When one human sees their own words and revelations captured and made real by another, the energetic connection of trust grows stronger. This simple act of service has helped them take the things in their mind that were lost in the chaos of their world and put them on paper. Re-reading the notes almost always leads to even more revelations for the client (and a pathway to the next steps in the deal).

So to review Mission 2:

1. **INTENTION:** GET IN POWER AND ALIGNMENT USING THE WEAPONS OF HEART, SPIRIT, AND BODY

2. **CONNECTION:** BRING THAT PRESENCE TO YOUR MEETING AND ORIENT THE OUTCOME TOWARD THE OTHER PERSON, AND "CREATE THE FIELD"

3. **REVELATION:** HOLD SPACE AND ASK THE MILLION-DOLLAR QUESTIONS

4. USE THE HACK OF WRITING VERBATIM NOTES DURING THE PROCESS TO STAY PRESENT, FOCUSED, AND PROTECT THE FIELD

5. **CREATION:** CLOSE THE LOOP OF CREATION AND RETURN THE NOTES TO THE OTHER PERSON

Now go find someone and run the play! 3, 2, 1…off you go!

RETURN & REPORT

How was your meeting? What difference did you notice about your own awareness? Did you see the elements of intention, connection, revelation, and creation emerge during the conversation? Were you aware of "the field" in space (and perhaps your own impulses to collapse it)?

It's important to know that this is not a game of perfection. It's a game of progress. The most important thing is that you are becoming aware of what is really going on both when a sales conversation is really great and when one falls apart. If you take this knowledge into your future sales engagement and commit to "being the most present man in the room," the results for your clients and the domination of your marketplace are only a matter of time.

What if I told you that there's someone that's holding space for you right now? As you are reading these words. At this very moment.

MISSION 3: RETURN TO THE CEO OF THE UNIVERSE

It's time to move on to the next MISSION and re-connect with the CEO of The Universe.

In The Weapon of The Spirit, you learned about the power of having gratitude and seeing His faithfulness over time as our "asks" are answered.

In The Weapon of the Heart, you learned about the power of linking the gift of your family to your production and mission.

In The Weapon of The Body, you learned about the concept of The Spiritual Warfare Protocol and how subjugating your body to physical exertion while listening to the Word of God humbles you and opens your heart.

Finally, In The Weapon of Presence, you learned about the power of holding space and being present, both in sales and in life.

In this mission, you're going to have a chance to bring it all together and connect with the fact that The CEO of The Universe is holding space for you. You're in His field and presence; you just need to be still to feel it.

All you need to connect with Him is the willingness to have a conversation.

I'm going to share a prayer meeting I had with God. It took place on a beach in Laguna Beach, CA, on November 20, 2019, while I was there to support the men of Warrior Week #62.

Early that morning, I had gotten up in the dark and completed my Spiritual Warfare Protocol. I had done "The Eric" (see Chapter 5) and listened to the book of Exodus during the session. That morning I had focused on this specific verse:

"Behold, I send an angel before you to guard you on the way and to bring you to the place that I have prepared. Pay careful attention to him and obey his voice; do not rebel against him, for he will not pardon your transgression, for my name is in him. But if you carefully obey his voice and do all that I say, then I will be an enemy to your enemies and an adversary to your adversaries."
- Exodus 23 : 20-22

Forty-five minutes after completing The Spiritual Warfare Protocol, I found myself on the beach alone in an open space with the waves gently coming in. I started praying and writing in my journal.

FROM MY JOURNAL:

11-20-19 - BEACH EVOLUTION,
Crystal Cove Beach, Laguna Beach, CA

God, my Father in Heaven...

I know you are here.

God, my Father in Heaven...I know you love me.

I love you.

Thank you for making the sun literally just shine on me! That was amazing! I can feel the warmth - I feel your love.

I know you love me. I know you are always with me. You have been shining a light on Coach Sam. Thank you for letting me see this.

I know you love it when your children listen and are obedient.

It honors you.

I don't feel like I've been listening or acting well enough. God, I am scared. I'm sorry.

I know you understand.

I cannot do any of this without you.

...I know that's the whole point.

Is this path the right one? I mean, the book, the platform, the beach - are these the things? Is there something else?

These seem like the right things. There seems to be something else.

I wonder what it is.

I know you will show me when it is time.

I wonder if I'm missing it.

But my eyes have not been opened yet. It is like what I want to see is on the other side of the island.

I'm scared.

But you have never brought me a gift that wasn't to my benefit.

Never.

I will hang in there. I know you have me.

Thank you, Father. Thank you for everything. My wife, my girls, continuing to heal Perry's feet, Your Son, The Spirit, Coach Sam, Brendan, my friend Eric* *(Eric had passed away just days before)

I know he is with you.

He was a good man.

He is yours.

Please comfort and take care of his wife and children.

I know you have them in your hand.

Please protect my wife and children. Guard them from darkness and evil and corruption.

I know you will.

Father, bring Coach Sam to know the Salvation of Jesus Christ.

I believe he is one of your Shepherds. He is following the path. I will support him.

He gave me such a gift at Warrior Week.

He helped me feel the weight of your Son's sacrifice.

Yes, God. Thank you.

So why should I fear anything?!

I shouldn't. You say "fear not" all the time.

It is hard. But following you is never the "easy" or "comfortable path."

Why am I here on this beach today?

I know it is to just focus on you. I would not have found this space for this.

I will take a picture. Thank you.

Why am I so scared to leap?

I cannot see the man you want me to be yet. I thought I could see him.

I know I haven't done the two things I feel called to do. The podcast AND the book. I have a feeling the podcast is helping more people than I know.

I worry that the numbers aren't high enough. I still hesitate to publish and market it.

I am afraid of someone.

Yes.

He is not someone to be afraid of. He is someone to pray for.

I pray that he finds you. Please bring him to you.

I will keep publishing the podcast.

I'm clear. What is the path to get the book done?

I feel like I should let Susanna read it.

I am confused about what to do with the editor, Bev.

I will talk to her.

Ok.

I'll also connect with Brendan's editor and get her to do a copy edit as a parallel path.

Wait.

There are no parallel paths with you.

So, just I'll talk to Bev.

Ok

I'm clear. What is the path to filming and getting the platform built? I feel called to go to LA during Dec 11 week with Jeremy (btw he is finding you.

I'm reminded of Dan Nagy's note. ("I will do anything.")

Am I over-thinking all of this?

I know I'm over thinking this.

LOL. Ahhhhh!

This is so frustrating. Please take my fear and uncertainty away.

I know you do. Every day. Then I invite it back.

Ahhhh!!!

Wow. There is literally "a family on the beach" walking my way from the right.

Wow

Ok.

I see..

Joy from the children. Running in the waves. No fear that it's cold. No fear of anything. They know their father is watching, and thus, they have no fear.

I know you're watching me. You are always present. I will keep following you. In you, I will not fall.

Lord - please send your Spirit and fill me up with it. Fill my cup. Set me on fire.

I feel like I already am. Send more. I saw the effect of the Word and workout on Brendan.

Yes.

There are many lost that need the Truth and the Light. I feel the push to go get them. To feed your sheep.

The island is clouded over now.

But I can still see the Light. You teach that sometimes it will be like this. Your Word says to have faith. Fear not. Others need to see a shepherd walk into the dark. If you never gave us some dark to work with - we wouldn't have a chance to bring the light.

Thank you for these opportunities, and please bless that family I just saw.

I know you will.

I see it.

I am are already "the man on the beach." I am already everything I need to be.

I'm literally on the beach right now!!!

And there is the irony!. :) Humor is from you too. Now I know why you wanted me to take a picture!

Parker is coming to get me.

I got the gift. I will GO AND SPREAD YOUR LIGHT.

I AM CLEAR.

-I LOVE YOU.

-End Journal Entry

MISSION ACTION PLAN

STEP 1: Start your morning in the Word of God and wait for a verse to stand out.

STEP 2: Find a quiet place, outside if possible.

STEP 3: Open your journal.

STEP 4: Start the meeting with two statements:

> "God, my father in heaven, I know you are here."
>
> "God, my father in heaven, I know you love me."
>
> Know that God hears you.
>
> Then, write whatever comes to your heart. Write what you hear in response. Continue for as long as you feel called. Repent. Thank. Ask. Seek. Knock.

STEP 5: When the meeting is complete, consider what things you were told to do. Write them down as actions.

STEP 6: Confirm that nothing you heard is in conflict with anything in scripture. God's direction **is never in conflict** with his Word.

STEP 7: Act. Go do what you were told to do and watch what happens.

RETURN & REPORT

That meeting on the beach in Laguna directly connects to you. If I didn't follow the instructions from that day, you would not be reading these words right now. There have been other things from that specific conversation in the presence of God that forever changed my life and the lives of many others.

My prayer and hope is that your experience with this mission reveals that you will always have the capacity to use the Weapon of Presence for others when you realize that The CEO of The Universe is present with you at every moment.

PROTOCOL

In addition to your weekly meetings with The CEO of the Universe, start having meetings with God as often as possible. He is waiting for you to seek, ask, knock, and act.

CONCLUSION

Ultimately sales, business, and family are all about creation. You have the choice to create from a place of ego-driven scarcity or divinely-inspired abundance. You have the choice to seek what you can get for yourself, or seek to be of service to others. You have a choice to worship idols or worship Him.

Using the Weapon of Presence gives you the ability to serve others as His instrument in your profession, whether in sales or another profession. It is a weapon for any mission field you are sent to fight.

As C.S. Lewis once wrote, "The question is not whether we should bring God into our work or not. We certainly should and must. The question is whether we should simply (a.) Bring Him in the dedication of our work to Him, in the integrity, diligence, and humility with which we do it, or also (b.) Make His professed and explicit service our job."

I challenge you to do both.

CHAPTER 8

WINNING THE SALES WAR

"Now therefore stand still and see this great thing

that the Lord will do before your eyes."

1 Samuel 12:16

Note to the reader: I was inspired to write this story about my daughter and when I went back and checked the day and time of the story below, I realized something amazing.

The following events took place on December 6, 2019 at 7:48AM and, in a miraculous confirmation of circumstance, this chapter was written exactly two years later to-the-minute at 7:48 AM on December 6, 2021.

WINNING THE SALES WAR

The last month of the sales year began, and I was not worried about the numbers.

The year had been profitable, and there were still deals that could come in before the end of the year. There was still pressure to close everything possible. Even still, I felt no pressure. I wasn't worried about my quota. I wasn't worried about bonuses. I wasn't even aware of who might be "Salesman of the Year." I did not care. Those idols were dead. *I was living beyond quota.* At this moment, I was only focused on one thing: the image of my daughter Perry sleeping with braces on her feet.

I was alone in the darkness of the gym and deep into a 600-rep Spiritual Warfare Protocol workout. The Gospel of Mark played through my headphones as I took on another round of burpees and pullups. I was circling Perry with reps. I could see her in my heart. She had been in casts or had worn braces every night of her life since the first treatment. It was the 1,010th night of wearing braces to treat her clubfeet. She had proven to be an absolute warrior. She never cried or complained about the braces. She just did the reps. Still, it hurt both my wife and me to lock her into them every night. The doctors had recently told us that when Perry takes off her braces herself, that she'd be close to the end of wearing them, but there were at least three to six more months to go.

As I saw her in my heart, I felt the same rage and power and love I did on that hill at Warrior Week. She was my fire. Every rep in the workout was a prayer. Every rep was a "thank you" to God. Every rep was a "will you" to God.

Then the following section of Mark started to powerfully resonate in my spirit:

> While he was still speaking, there came from the ruler's house some who said, "Your daughter is dead. Why trouble the Teacher any further?" But overhearing what they said, Jesus said to the ruler of the synagogue, "Do not fear, only believe." And he allowed no one to follow him except Peter and James and John the brother of James. They came to the house of the ruler of the synagogue, and Jesus saw a commotion, people weeping and wailing loudly. And when he had entered, he said to them, "Why are you making a commotion and weeping? The child is not dead but sleeping." And they laughed at him. But he put them all outside and took the child's father and mother and those who were with him and went in where the child was. Taking her by the hand he said to her, "Talitha cumi," which means, "Little girl, I say to you, arise." And immediately the girl got up and began walking (for she was twelve years of age), and they were immediately overcome with amazement. - Mark 5:35-42

"Talitha Cumi"

I fell to my knees in the gym as those words came through.

"Little girl, I say to you, arise."

I started sobbing, overwhelmed with the words of Jesus as he told the little girl to arise and "begin walking." I prayed this prayer and asked him with every rep to do the same for Perry.

I sent Susanna a text with the Bible verse from Mark and a picture of Perry along with a little "sobbing" emoji.

A minute later, she sent me a text back.

"She just took her shoe off."

Susanna was watching her on the baby monitor camera that looked down into her crib.

"Wtf"

"Shoes off. She's on the move!" sent Susanna.

"I have been listening to this verse over and over again for the last 30 minutes."

"Oh, they are both off now!"

"This is a divine moment. Immediately overcome with amazement. Take a picture of her!"

As I was on my knees in tears, sobbing, I realized something and sent another text.

"This is the last day of her braces."

I grabbed my keys and rushed home to see the living example of God's faithfulness that is my family.

Not by might nor by power, but by My Spirit, - Zechariah 4:6

The first three weapons bring awareness to three core areas of your being: your connection to God, your connection to your family, and your connection to yourself. Each weapon gives you a process to go to war with the darkness that comes from disconnection. As you've used the weapons, missions, and protocols, you have been experiencing not only *awareness* but *presence* within each of these areas.

This is exactly what I was experiencing the morning Perry took off her braces.

The weapons are the gateways to creating more power, more connection, and more capacity with yourself, your family, and with God so that you can be more, so you can bring more. When you use the weapons, you will shift from the victim to the victor.

You are called to live a life beyond the systems of the world. You are called to be in the world, but not of it. It is key to living beyond your quota, beyond your fear, beyond scarcity. It is the pathway to "knowing" that you can create, even when you cannot see the path. It is to surrender and rest in God.

There's a bigger, cosmic battle at work here that goes beyond having power for your next presentation. It's the battle for ALIGNMENT.

There is an energetic thread that runs from where you are now to the next most sanctified version of yourself. There is an infinite number of possibilities of who you could become, but have you ever asked who you are called to become?

Most simply drift.

Most men drift in and out of darkness for their entire lives and "end up" being one of the potential versions by default. That version might be in the light or in the dark, but he is never The Light In The Dark.

The war begins when a man understands exactly who he is; he strips off labels of salesman, rainmaker, or Salesman of The Year and leaves them in the past.

At any given moment, He is either heading towards ALIGNMENT or OUT OF ALIGNMENT. He is either SEEKING ALIGNMENT or SEEKING DARKNESS.

But alignment to what? Our purpose? Our calling? Our passion? These are just popular names for alignment to **God's Will.**

We are all being called forth to be the next-most-sanctified version of ourselves.

It is an eternal game of death and renewal. The man you are today must die to become the man that God is calling you to be. This is the process that began for me on that hill in Warrior Week. Perhaps this book has already begun that process in you. Even if it's only because you know one thing now: YOU ARE NOT ALONE.

In the years that followed, I was called to serve as a Warrior Week coach alongside Coach Sam Falsafi. As Warrior Week #67 approaches in 2022, we have seen this process play out hundreds of times.

When men become aligned, there is an exponential increase in power and clarity. Men transform. Their bodies look and operate differently. Their desire to commune daily with God becomes non-negotiable. Marriages and relationships with children flourish. Men stop chasing business and start attracting it.

Every conflict in our lives comes down to a simple question:

Whose desires and will am I seeking? Who is my god? Myself or my Father in Heaven?

Faced with the impending torture and crucifixion, Jesus Christ acknowledged His own human will while seeking God's Will.

"Father, if you are willing, remove this cup from me. Nevertheless, not my will, but yours, be done." - Luke 22:42

This book was borne out of my own desire to intentionally seek God's will. In December of 2017, deep in prayer, I was given three simple instructions: Launch a podcast. Publish the book. Wait for further instructions.

The podcast took me nearly a year to launch and was finally launched in October 2018. The book took me four years. I wrote the first page on a flight in December 2017. During these four years, all of my own personal struggle was out of a war with certainty and worthiness to write and broadcast.

It was the resistance that comes when a man seeks alignment.

There will always be resistance.

Furthermore, the actions of the man seeking alignment will always seem strange and unusual to those who are out of alignment or seeking their own will over God's.

Being a salesman is one of the toughest and most rewarding professions on the planet. Living in this world can destroy a man. It destroys a lot of men and a lot of families. But now you have a choice. How will you operate?

Will you shift your life, or will you remain status quo? (You are kind of stuck. Now that you have this knowledge, to take it and *not apply it* would be a crime against yourself.) All liability is now yours. You must decide.

What will you choose? Will you worship or destroy your idols?

Go to war. I **challenge you** to be more.

BONUS CHAPTER

THE FORMULA FOR GUARANTEED RESULTS

THE FORMULA FOR GUARANTEED RESULTS

You've gained some knowledge from the book, and my hope is that you've been running the missions and protocols during your journey. Congrats on making it this far! I'm going to give you the four keys to a formula that, when followed, guarantees results in any area of life if you play all in.

1. Select an established proven process: This is not a time to invent something for the first time if you want to GUARANTEE results. An established and proven path must be in place for you to follow.

2. Find a guide/coach who has walked the path you seek: No hero goes on a Hero's Journey without a guide. Luke Skywalker had Obi-Wan. Even Michael Jordan had a coach. You must have someone who has actually WALKED the path you are seeking before walking alongside you.

3. Make a meaningful investment: There is nothing like putting your money where your mouth is to set a frame on yourself. Any journey that involves growth will come with some level of pain and discomfort. There will be days where you don't want to do anything, but it will be those days that you'll remember the money you invested and go anyway. Money is also an energetic exchange, and "free"

training never works long term because there is not an exchange of energy. Always pay your Guide/Coach for YOUR sake.

4. Surround the outcome with brotherhood and accountability: The Spartan phalanx was one of the most powerful tactics in military history because of the commitment between each man to protect the man next to him. When a man realizes that when he does not meet commitments to himself that he is giving everyone else permission to drop their own shields, that liability is what will keep him in the game. Many times, we won't do the hard things for ourselves, but we'll do it because we don't want to let our brothers down.

If you want guaranteed results in any area of life, make sure you put these four frameworks in place around the target.

BONUS CHAPTER

LEAD WHAT
YOU LIVE

LEAD WHAT YOU LIVE

There are thousands of books on sales tips, tricks, and tactics. There are a million cold call scripts, presentation templates, and negotiation tactics. The truth is, the reason sales has a bad rap is that men, in general, are a shit show. If you want to be a better salesman, you have to be a better man first.

Becoming a better man begins with leadership and personal integrity. Whether you are a CEO, VP, sales manager, pastor, father, or husband, your capacity to lead your company, your team or your family is 100% proportional to your ability to lead yourself. If you can't lead yourself, don't expect anyone to follow you.

In fact, a man who fails to lead himself is like a ship that "will be tossed to and fro by every wind." Like a boat in the ocean, as he tries to make progress, he doesn't create an energetic wake that positively impacts others. Instead, he creates a whirlpool. He creates a never-ending loop of burn and rise, destroy and survive. He not only drowns himself but pulls down his team, customers, and even his family into that maelstrom.

There is a simple and fundamental problem with most leaders in most companies: they are trying to lead from a place they do not live. Unless you are LIVING something, you will always lack integrity in your leadership.

I used to do this at home, where I would read a book, get fired up about the knowledge I was learning, and then encourage my wife that she should follow whatever protocol I had just learned. You can imagine how that went over. You may have done this or probably experienced this within your company.

"Read this new sales book and do everything in it."

Punch yourself in the face.

At this point, I would encourage you to LIVE some of the things you have LEARNED in this book before you try and lead anyone in any of these practices. LIVE these practices, and I can guarantee you that you will get results. People will begin to FOLLOW because of your results, not because of your words.

Brother, there is power in you, and the world needs men that are taking a stand.

Lead from what you live.

Let your life be your first ministry.

THE END.

WEAPONS
AND RESOURCES

WEAPONS AND RESOURCES

THE FOUR WEAPONS OF THE SALES WAR: MASTER CLASS

Are you ready to go deeper into The Sales War? This experiential online training curriculum expands on all of the weapons in this book in a multi-week experience to weaponize you across www.thesaleswar.com

THE SALES WEAPONIZATION PROTOCOL: MASTER CLASS

If James Bond and the Matrix joined together to make a B2B sales curriculum this is what you would get. Learn all of the fundamentals and weapons that will allow you to dominate sales in any industry in this *full spectrum* experiential online training course. This is not your mama's sales training. Become a sales assassin.

www.thesaleswar.com

THE SALES WARRIOR PODCAST - Apple / Spotify / Google

As your host every week, Brian shares his 20 years of sales experience along with insights and strategies from amazing guests to be your guide in accessing your ultimate sales weapon…your heart.

www.thesaleswar.com

WARRIOR WEEK

The most elite training for married businessmen on the planet. By application only: www.warriorweek.com

WORK WITH COACH BQ:

Revenue strategy & consulting for the weaponization of B2B sales teams. By application only: ***www.thesaleswar.com***

OTHER RESOURCES:

ADIDAS TRAINING APP: www.runtastic.com/

YOUVERSION BIBLE APP: www.youversion.com/

CHATBOOKS: www.chatbooks.com

QUANTUM APP (This book would not have been completed without this deep work app. Special Thanks to Jeremy Finlay.)

www.joinquantum.com

SPIRITUAL FURY SPOTIFY PLAYLIST:
www.thesaleswar.com/weapons

FOLLOW BQ on INSTAGRAM: www.instagram.com/ brianqdavis12/

RECOMMENDED BOOKS:

- THE HOLY BIBLE – EVERY ANSWER IS FOUND HERE.

- PITCH ANYTHING by OREN KLAFF

- FLIP THE SCRIPT by OREN KLAFF

- EVERY MAN A LEADER by SAM FALSAFI

- THE 15 FUNDAMENTAL LAWS OF DE-ESCALATION
  by BRENDAN KING

- WHAT IF WE'VE BEEN DOING IT ALL WRONG?
  by ERIC L DUNAVANT

- BUCK ACADEMY (Children's book)
  by DUSTIN & FEBYOLLA GOSS

- DANGEROUS PRAYERS by CRAIG GROESCHEL

- HUSBANDS & FATHERS by DEREK PRINCE

GRATITUDE AND ACKNOWLEDGEMENTS

The following individuals have directly contributed to my life and, in some way, this book. I am deeply grateful for their love, belief, and support during my journey in life, sales and with God.

J.Q. DAVIS

SUZANNAH DAVIS (REST IN PEACE)

GORDON NELSON (REST IN PEACE)

PRISCILLA DAVIS

SALLY THOMAS

RON THOMAS

SAM FALSAFI

GARRET J WHITE

OREN KLAFF

JEREMY FINLAY

PASTOR RORY CLARK

PASTOR MIKE FABAREZ

PATRICK MARK

ALETHA REIL

MIKE REIL

BRENDAN KING

BRENT KOCAL

CHRIS BALLARD

DAVID FEDOR

DON SCHULTZ

DUSTIN LUCE

DUSTIN GOSS

JASON KEHLER

JB BRANGERS

JEFF OLDROYD

JEREMIAH RIVERS

JOE KESSI

KEN KOTCH

KEVIN PALKA

LEE CREWSON

MATT RADMACHER

SCOTT RAYMER

ERIC DUNAVANT

TONY CHIARELLI

PATRICK BOSCASSY

AARON HOWARD

ROD THOMAS

ED JACKSON

DAN BEDELL

JONO SCOTT

PATRICK FLOOD

JEREMY NELSON

JAMIE ADAMS

RUSTIN KRETZ

BRIAN COX

ERIN DELONY

CHRIS CRIPPS

LARRY KUEHN

DAVE SHIELDS

SAM ABU HAMDAN

CHRIS VISNIC

SHAWN NELSON

MAX DAVIS

JON & CORI IANODISI

STEPHEN PARTRICK

DERIC KELLER

MARK MACINERNY

JASON & JENNIE SMITH

DANIEL BERGER

FRANCO CABRAL

NICK SCARABOSIO

ASHLIE WALTON

JILL & TOBY RIDER

BRAD & SARAH DAVIS

JULIE NELSON

KEVIN NELSON

BERTHA DAVIS (REST IN PEACE)

SKEET DAVIS

JIMMY VREELAND

SAMUEL NEIDER

SUNDEE CORLEY

COACH STEVE TRICHE

LUDGER HEMESATH

JASON HARRIMAN

NED ARICK

NEGIN FALSAFI

SUE REESE FINLAY

SEVERIN FENDERHEN

JASON BRINK

CHERRYL TURNER

THOMAS MURPHY

DAN NAGY

DR. OMAR IBRAHIM

DESIREE CHAMBERLAIN

JONATHAN CHAMBERLAIN

LOURDES GANT

BOYD CAMPBELL

MEILANI VENEY

BRANDON GRANT

DAVID PLAISANCE

EVELYN MENEGHIN

JACIE GREEN

JENNIFER SCHULTZ

TORY SMITH

BYRON ROSE

LOGAN LAPOSTA

MIKEE LINTON

BERNARDO LUCENA

MIKE FALLAT

MICHAEL BUFFINGTON

CULLEN TALLEY

DR. DAVID BOYD

SCOTT STOLTZ

PARKER WHITE

STEVEN PRESSFIELD

BRANDON MATHESON

DAVE MEYER

EPHREM JANDO

JAMES FAUGHTENBERRY

JEAN-PAUL WRIGHT

JEAN-PHILLIPE GAGNE

JENNINGS DEPRIEST

JOHNNY BOCOBO

JOSH MCDERMOTT

CHRIS BEALL

THE MEN OF WARRIOR WEEK #38

COREY QUINN

CODY CHULA

SOPHIA MURPHY

RYAN NIDDEL

CHRISTINE BRELLO

KIRK VITRY

ANDY SCHRECK

KATRINA JOHNSON

LAURA METRO

MICHAEL SAUER

JORDAN WILSON

RANDELL CLARKE

JOHN GILMORE

DEMIAN LICHTENSTEIN

DAVID J WOOD

BO BUTLER

TOM TOMLO

TERENCE MITCHELL (RIP)

COACH THOMAS DELAUER

BART SCHAD

BRIAN HOLLOWAY

DAVID STORER

ERIC CERWIN (REST IN PEACE)

FORREST WALDEN

GERRITT BAKE

JACE YOUNG

JEFF TILLEY

JOSH VELLA

KEVIN VOISIN

MARC UGO

MICHAEL TIRIKOS

RUSS PERRY

SHAHN ELLIS

THOMAS DOUGLAS

THOMAS MIFSUD

TYLER BELL

DAN BEDNARSKI

JESSE EWELL

JEFF MCGREGOR

DEDICATION

This book is dedicated to Susanna, Annie Grace, and Perry. You are my loves. You are my lights. You are my fire. Without you, I would not be who I am. Your sacrifice and love made it possible to get this message to other men in the dark.

You are my Divine Gift.

I love you.

BQD

SPECIAL THANKS

Special thanks to Aletha Reil, my final editor, whose spirit-driven editing and encouragement were the catalyst to bring this book into reality. You and Mike are an answered prayer.

Special thanks to Dr. David Fedor and Jason "JB" Brangers for your spiritual counsel.

Your zealotry for the The Word of Truth is an edifying joy.

YOUR NOTES & REVELATIONS

YOUR NOTES & REVELATIONS

YOUR NOTES & REVELATIONS

YOUR NOTES & REVELATIONS

ABOUT THE AUTHOR

Brian Q. Davis has been a B2B sales executive for over 20 years across industries as diverse as aerospace and defense, enterprise software, digital marketing, and healthcare.

He is a practicing sales executive, coach and trainer in personal development, sales, storytelling, strategy and the arts of pitching, presentation and presence-based selling. He is the founder of The Sales Warrior Podcast and creator of The Sales Weaponization Protocol training curriculum.

He finds his greatest joy in changing the trajectories of people.

He is also a Warrior Week Coach and a pastor at a small church in Dallas, TX, where he lives with his wife and two daughters.

Contact:
brianqdavis@thesaleswar.com

www.thesaleswar.com

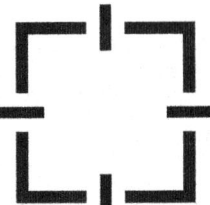

Made in the USA
Middletown, DE
12 October 2022